# EATING DISORDERS | *Helping Your Child Recover*

*Edited by*
Steve Bloomfield

*Published by*
Eating Disorders Association

**Eating Disorders:** *Helping Your Child Recover*

Edited by
Steve Bloomfield

Published by
Eating Disorders Association,
103 Prince of Wales Road,
Norwich, NR1 1DW

First published 2006

ISBN10: 0-9551772-1-9

ISBN13: 978-0-9551772-1-7

---

This book is not intended to replace treatment or advice by a qualified health professional and the publishers will not accept any responsibility for any actions or consequences arising out of the use or misuse of this book.

Book design by Graham Land Creative Services Wymondham
Cover by Allsopp Davies Norwich
Printed by Page Bros Norwich

# Acknowledgements

Thank you to all the carers, sufferers and professionals involved in the treatment of eating disorders for being so generous with their time and for giving us permission to use their quotations, as well as to the helpline workers at EDA who have helped to guide this work from the very start.

Special thanks must also go to Jade McEwen and Sally Marais, whose hard work made this book a reality; without them and their efforts there would be no book.

# Eating Disorders Association (EDA)

This book is published by the Eating Disorders Association, the UK charity supporting people with eating disorders.

EDA offers support and information about eating disorders to sufferers, carers and professionals. EDA runs nationally recognised helplines for adults and young people and supports a UK-wide network of self help groups. The website at www.edauk.com is recognised by NHS Direct and provides a huge resource of information and access to message board and other services. EDA offers a range of other services and information including; training, education programmes, booklets and leaflets on different aspects of eating disorders.

Throughout this book we will make reference to EDA services which we believe would be of help to you, your family and the young people in your care. Full details of our services and how to obtain them appear in the Appendix at the end of the book.

# Contents

# Helping Your Child Recover

*Eating Disorders: Helping Your Child Recover* is about caring for a teenager with an eating disorder. This book is for parents, carers, guardians and anyone else with parental responsibility. We have all of you in mind whenever we refer to 'parents'.

We begin with some information to help you understand eating disorders. We hope this will add to your understanding and empower you to support your child more confidently. In later chapters you will learn how an eating disorder can affect your child, yourself and the rest of your family. We consider how you and your family can work together to maintain a sense of normality while you tackle the eating disorder. Caring for your child will be challenging; we offer suggestions that we hope will help you to care effectively. We conclude with chapters on some of the medical aspects of an eating disorder, their treatment and recovery, followed by details of useful contacts mentioned in the text.

Parents were involved in preparing this book; their thoughts, feelings and experiences are quoted in italics throughout the text. The special insight and honesty these comments reveal should help you feel less alone in your family's struggle and more positive about your ability to cope.

Many people with an eating disorder will be able to recover with the support of professionals, without going into hospital as an inpatient, and there is growing evidence that outpatient treatment with the support of the family is one of the most effective ways for young people to recover from an eating disorder. You and your family play a vital role in achieving a healthy recovery because of the love and support you give your child. Many recovered sufferers have told us how important their families were during the fight to get well. Extracts from their accounts of living with an eating disorder are included at the end of Chapter One.

You might decide to read the book straight through; you might prefer to turn to the chapters that seem most relevant at the moment. At times the parents' comments will be comforting to refer to; at other times the young sufferers' views will attract your attention. Perhaps some of you will personalise the book, adding your own thoughts, questions and dated observations; you could annotate the text, attach sticky notes to pages that are of special interest, or write notes on the blank pages at the back of the book.

As a parent all you want is for your child to recover. We want our book to help you with this, but we hope it will help you to look after yourself, too.

Finally, and most importantly, through all the achievements and setbacks you will experience with a young person affected by an eating disorder, it is important to remember that recovery is always possible.

## Editor's note

We have decided to avoid the usual practice of writing as if the sufferer is female; we hope you will forgive the occasional clumsiness that results from this decision. For the sake of simplicity throughout the book we have used the term *anorexia* instead of the full medical term *anorexia nervosa* and *bulimia* rather than *bulimia nervosa*.

Contact details for all the organisations mentioned in the text, along with the EDA helpline numbers, e-mail and web addresses are in the Appendix at the end of the book.

# CHAPTER ONE

# Understanding eating disorders

Here we explain what might be going on in your child's mind. You are introduced to the inner voice that will resent and resist parental efforts to combat the illness. We outline the stages of an eating disorder and we urge you to find ways of communicating your own concerns if you are worried about your child. At the end of this chapter five young people speak; we hope their words will enhance your understanding.

## Why do young people develop eating disorders?

Eating disorders enable young people to block out or control painful thoughts and feelings which they have been unable to cope with. Sufferers can be deeply affected by a range of issues, pressures and significant events: a common factor is loss of self-esteem.

These issues may include bullying and teasing, especially about weight or body shape, abuse of any kind, whether emotional, physical or sexual and coping with bereavement and loss. Pressures can come from others, including the pressure to succeed academically or to conform socially; there may also have been pressure to lose weight from friends, family, GP or the media. Young people can also pressure themselves, especially if they are perfectionists. A poor body image can torment a teenager, even when no one else can see a problem and there is no teasing. Difficulties with relationships, especially in the making and keeping of friends, can cause deep unhappiness. There are unavoidable life events, involving change or transition, such as puberty, moving from primary to secondary school and leaving school for university, further education or work. For some, attitudes towards food and eating acquired during childhood can have an impact later in life.

Every experience of an eating disorder is unique to the individual; the causes will vary too. The list above is not exhaustive and many items will not apply to your child, who probably does not know why this has happened. Research shows that for some people there is a genetic reason why they may be prone to developing an eating disorder. Specialists call this a genetic predisposition. This may affect only one family member or occasionally all family members.

> *I have an eating disorder. Saying this to your family is terrifying. Automatically your parents want an explanation. There really isn't one, above and beyond the fact that I am not happy with myself. I wanted to make it clear to them that they had nothing to do with it. This was about me. It's going to take time to work through this, but hopefully I will get there.* JOSIE, 18

Working out how to tackle the eating disorder right now is more helpful than worrying about why it started. Whatever the reasons, your child did not choose to become unwell or intend to worry you so much. As Josie's comments above indicate, persisting with questions that cannot be answered will frustrate you and perhaps make your child less willing to talk about other aspects of the eating disorder.

## What does it feel like to have an eating disorder?

When someone you love is affected by an eating disorder, it is only natural for you to wonder what it must feel like. You might think that if you knew what it felt like you could understand the illness better. However, even if you have suffered from an eating disorder yourself, you will not necessarily know what your own child is feeling. Bear in mind, too, how annoying it can be when someone tries to tell you that they 'know just how you feel'.

**Young people give us some insight in these comments about their eating disorder:**

*It makes me feel protected and in control.*

*I like myself better when I have less fat on my body.*

*I don't have to think about anything else when I'm hungry.*

*Bingeing blocks everything out for a while, but then I usually feel guilty.*

*I eat too much food in an attempt to make myself feel better.*

In each case the sufferer believes that the eating disorder makes them feel better. This must be hard for you to accept when you can see how harmful it is. If you are to be effective in the recovery process, you do need to understand just how afraid your child feels about life without the disorder.

*I try to support my daughter who has anorexia, but it's hard for me to understand why she has it when I have never experienced anything like it. It does not make sense to me, but I suppose it doesn't have to. There is no rationalising something like this – it's impossible.* MARGARET

## HOW CAN YOU HELP?

- If this is new to you, as it was for Margaret, find out all you can. You have already made a start with this book. We hope that what you read here will gradually begin to make some sense of what you are observing and experiencing at home.

- Remember that you are still the expert on your child. The teenage years can be mystifying and confusing for many parents and sometimes the young person seems like a stranger. An eating disorder complicates this period, but there is probably no one who knows more about your child than you.

- You can empathise with your child, but many of the thoughts and feelings arising from their eating disorder will seem irrational or illogical to you. They may insist that they are fat when you know they are severely underweight: you do not have to agree with them, but you can begin to accept that this is what they really feel and believe.

## In two minds

Young people often think about their eating disorder in two very different and contradictory ways. They are literally 'in two minds'. In one state of mind they are desperate to break free from their eating disorder and determined to seek help. In the other state of mind the prospect of living without the eating disorder fills them with terror. This can be confusing for them and for their families.

> *There were small glimpses in time where my daughter would talk about getting help. She would discuss it with me, but then not want to take it any further. I tried not to push the issue too much because she would get very frustrated towards me. Her temperament would completely change, I felt like I had to back off.* JANE

You can imagine how Jane's spirits lifted when her daughter first spoke positively about getting help and how disappointed she felt when the subject had to be dropped for a while. However, it is clear that as Jane gradually learned to recognise which state of mind was uppermost, she was able to adapt her responses accordingly.

We can all be *in two minds* about important issues in our lives: most of us know how painful it can be to make difficult, life-changing decisions when there is no certainty about the outcome. However, we are aware of this inner turmoil and we will eventually make up our mind. Sometimes, when a young person is in the grip of an eating disorder, the negative state of mind takes over so completely that the sufferer loses touch with other ways of thinking.

## The 'voice'

Eating disorders can have such a powerful influence on young sufferers that many will refer to the *voice* of their disorder. *This voice is a common experience for eating disorder sufferers; it is always on the side of the eating disorder.* This is an extreme extension of the negative state of mind. The *voice* can be harsh, critical, demanding, persuasive and extremely persistent; it is very real and very frightening to sufferers and seems to direct their thinking and behaviour. This may help you to understand why your child seems like a stranger at times. The *voice* is a bully and it will be particularly loud whenever parents and healthcare professionals seem to threaten the eating disorder. Many sufferers are afraid to acknowledge or refer to this *voice* for fear that it may be confused with a feature of some other serious mental health problems or psychoses where people experience other personalities talking to them, forcing them to do inappropriate things.

## HOW CAN YOU HELP?

- You are right to feel encouraged if your child talks about getting help. At least they have acknowledged that there is a problem. Be cautious, though, reminding yourself that this may just have been an attempt to please you. Even if the desire for help seemed heartfelt at the time, be prepared for a complete change of mind the next time you talk. The *voice* will have been at work on your child in the meantime.

- Remember that your child will remain convinced for a long time that the eating disorder makes them feel better, even when the more unpleasant symptoms are affecting them quite badly. Talk of recovery is a world away from the reality of treatment. Letting your child know that you understand this will help them feel safer in sharing their very confusing feelings with you.

- As you become more aware of the two minds that seem to operate within your child, you will become more confident in helping your child to recognise them too. Perhaps in time you can work together to challenge the views of the *voice*, which is always on the side of the eating disorder.

- Teenagers can be difficult and are sometimes quite rude. As parents of a teenager with an eating disorder, you will sometimes feel, rightly, that you are getting more than your fair share of such behaviour. Remember it is the disorder that is making your child behave in this way. It is particularly important to take time to tell your child how much you love them and how much they mean to you, when you feel calm enough to mean what you say.

## The development of an eating disorder

To recover from an eating disorder the sufferer has to be ready to make and accept changes in their behaviour. The following stages help to explain how attitudes to change develop; this may help you to understand your child's readiness to change and therefore work towards recovery. Professionals have identified a number of key stages in the sufferer's attitude towards their eating disorder. These stages are often referred to in these terms: precontemplation, contemplation, determination and action, and maintenance. These stages form a cycle of behaviour which the sufferer may pass through more than once in the recovery process, perhaps returning to one particular stage several times.

## Pre-contemplation

At this stage sufferers usually have no thoughts about change, and are dependent on their eating disorder, which is seen as a solution to their problems, offering many rewards and very few unpleasant consequences. They are in denial: they do not believe they have a problem so there is absolutely nothing to worry about.

## Contemplation

At this stage sufferers are in two minds about their eating disorder. They can see how damaging it is but they can also see many rewards in maintaining it: the prospect of life without the eating disorder is daunting. These opposing attitudes make the sufferer very confused about what they want.

## Determination and Action

At this stage sufferers believe that life would be better without their eating disorder. They are ready to commit to change, and begin working seriously towards recovery.

## Maintenance

After change has been made, sufferers face the daunting task of maintaining recovery. They have to manage the demands and frustrations of life without their old coping mechanism. This stage is extremely challenging. Sufferers who learn positive alternative coping strategies during treatment and receive long-term support will have a good chance of maintaining recovery, but they are still likely to struggle at times. Others will relapse into the comfort and familiarity of their eating disorder if they have not been prepared for this stage, and will move to a modified pre-contemplation state.

You have probably already identified the stage you believe your child to be at right now. Perhaps they seem to be between stages. Making the transition from one stage to the next can take a long time and may be difficult to observe. It is common for the sufferer to go through some or all of these stages several times before they recover fully from their eating disorder. It is most important that you accept this, so that you can be ready for your child's disappointment and frustration when this happens. It is only a setback: it is not a failure.

> *I think it's really important for other parents to realise that it may take their child several attempts at trying to get better before they actually do. It's also important to say that change does not happen overnight. It takes a long time. I wish I had known this when my daughter's eating problems started.*
> IDA

Ida was not prepared for this frustrating and exhausting aspect of the recovery process. Young people who experience a relapse after a period of maintained recovery are sometimes afraid to let their parents know, for fear of disappointing or even angering them. They may even feel that they have let their parents down by 'failing', label themselves as failures and give up trying.

## HOW CAN YOU HELP?

- You can help by being realistic whenever there are signs that your child is moving forward to the next stage. Show your delight, offer support and encouragement, but prepare yourself for a setback. If it comes it will be hard for your child, but they will cope better when they see that you are able to accept this without being unduly surprised or disappointed.

- You cannot force or hurry your child through any of these stages: dates and deadlines have no relevance here. Readiness for change must come from them if real recovery is to be achieved and maintained. However, they do need to feel supported and strengthened by your love, encouragement and understanding. Appropriate professional input can be a vital factor and we look at this in Chapter Six.

## Voicing your concerns

Perhaps you have been worried about your child for some time, but thought you might be overreacting to behaviour and comments arising, for example, from their decision to become vegetarian or to try a particular diet. You now feel sure that you are observing signs of an eating disorder, you think of little else but you do not know what to do next. Should you voice your concerns? If you do, what sort of reaction might you get?

Consider whether your personal view of your child may need to change in order to respect and value the person your child has become, as they fight their eating disorder.

> *After talking to my son about my concerns, I would walk away feeling like I was the one with the problem. He had logical answers for everything I would ask him about, and what he said really did make sense to me. The problem was that I knew something was wrong, and I could not stop thinking that although he made perfect sense, he wasn't telling me everything.* SHANE

Shane decided to speak to his son, who sounds bright, articulate and forceful. He wanted his father to leave him alone and he achieved this with a very persuasive response. Shane, however, could not shake off his belief that *something was wrong*, whatever his son said. That first approach must have been very difficult, but it was also very important. Shane had voiced his concerns: his son had heard them.

### HOW CAN YOU HELP?

- Eating disorders do need to be challenged, so the sooner you find the courage to do this the better for everyone involved. Think in terms of voicing concerns rather than seeking a confrontation. Aim to be clear about your concerns, based on what you've noticed yourself and what you've found out elsewhere. Refer to Chapter Five for guidance on signs of eating disorders. There is no need to mention eating disorders during the initial approach; just make sure that your child understands that you are worried about their physical and emotional health.

- Think ahead about details, such as the best time and situation for speaking to your child. If there are two parents, decide whether you should both be present and who should speak first. Work out a time when you and your child are likely to be reasonably calm, when no one is about to go out and when interruptions, such as other children bursting into the room, can be minimised. Avoid mealtimes. Think about how to begin, so your child doesn't feel immediately threatened and refuse to listen at all. Talking to a helpline worker at EDA might be useful at this point, especially if you are on your own.

● However your child reacts, a start has been made. If there is an eating disorder, your involvement has made the prospect of recovery much more likely and you may have gained insight into their current state of mind from the reactions you get. If you discover that there is genuinely another explanation, at least eating disorders have been eliminated.

● Be ready for a variety of reactions. Shane's son offered logical answers but you might encounter anger, disbelief, shock, amusement, concern for your welfare, denial, relief or perhaps refusal to engage at all. You may have to return to your concerns another day, but at least your child knows what they are.

● Remind yourself that eating disorders make the sufferer feel in control and able to cope with life, so any apparent threat to the disorder will put them on the defensive. Happy, healthy teenagers can be highly resistant to parental interference at the best of times but resistance will be fiercer when fuelled by an eating disorder. Uncomfortable questions may be bitterly resented, and the sufferer will always have a reasonable excuse for everything you express concern about.

● If you get far enough to suggest making an appointment with the GP, be aware that this will be a massive step for many young people. Immediate refusal probably indicates real fear or even an inability to see any need for this. You might leave this for another occasion. Voicing your concerns for the first time is difficult enough.

## Why doesn't your child want help?

*I found it really frustrating to sit there and watch my daughter slowly wither away. I could not understand how even after diagnosis she would not accept help. She simply did not want to try. This made me feel very helpless. If she did not want to help herself, how could I be expected to help her?* JULIA

Julia's daughter is clearly ill but still refusing help. Much has happened since Julia voiced her concerns: a professional diagnosis has been made and it sounds as if treatment has been offered. Julia and her daughter have made significant progress but that is not how it feels to either of them. This parent feels 'very helpless' and her daughter's health continues to deteriorate.

You know that eating disorders serve a purpose, enabling sufferers to feel better about themselves by providing a coping and control mechanism. It is the fear of being without this that causes fierce resistance to help of any kind, however advanced the eating disorder is in its effects. Only when the sufferer really wants change will help be more readily accepted, perhaps even asked for and welcomed.

## HOW CAN YOU HELP?

● You will feel helpless whenever your child is *stuck* but remember that when nothing seems to be changing externally, the *two minds* might be engaged in a real struggle. You might find opportunities to challenge the negative thinking and to encourage the positive, especially if you stay calm whichever state of mind is uppermost.

● You will continue to be helpful as you offer practical care on a daily basis, find out more about eating disorders, observe your child, perhaps make notes of what you learn and maybe keep a diary where you can focus on your own feelings.

● Accept that you cannot make your child want to get better; that is their responsibility. As a parent, however, your instinct is to protect your children from harm because you love them and feel responsible for them. These conflicting attitudes towards recovery might be easier to live with if acknowledged openly.

● It is possible, and sometimes necessary, to insist that a younger sufferer does accept treatment, against their wishes, especially if the illness becomes life-threatening. There is more on treatment in Chapter Six, but it is worth mentioning here that if treatment is undertaken resentfully, or only to please you, recovery may take longer. However, young people who have recovered will often say, 'I'm really pleased my mum made me go the doctor's – I'd never have gone on my own.'

● Encourage your child at receptive moments to tell you of changes and improvements they have noticed, however small. Acknowledge and welcome them, adding your own observations, too. However, you should not focus on weight gain.

● Talk about ordinary things: school, friends, siblings (brothers and sisters), pets, any special talents, interests and ambitions your child has, music, what's on television, what's in the news and anything else that will give you both a break from the eating disorder and draw you back into the real world. Think of this as bait to tempt and encourage your child's more positive state of mind – and yours.

## Recovering

People can and do recover from eating disorders.

Many of you will eventually see your child make a full recovery. Most of you will see at least partial recovery: your child will learn to manage their eating disorder, using techniques learned in treatment. Your child's health will be greatly improved, perhaps even fully restored, once recovery is maintained.

> *I don't think our daughter will ever be really comfortable around food. She has recovered from an eating disorder, but she continues to have rigid views about what she will and won't eat. She sticks to what she considers to be healthy foods and healthy portions. She maintains a healthy weight and seems to be determined not to go back to her eating disorder.* SALLY

No two cases are the same. Some young people will recover in a few months; others may need several years with a number of attempts at recovery. A few will remain very ill. When early diagnosis is followed up quickly by appropriate treatment, the chances of a healthy recovery are relatively high. Eating disorders can leave recovered sufferers vulnerable to relapses but good treatment programmes will teach them how to recognise the signs in future and take evasive action.

Sadly, anorexia has a higher death rate than any other mental health problem. Occasionally anorexia can be fatal, either from suicide or from the effects of prolonged starvation, in particular heart failure. However, the risk of premature death reduces significantly once treatment has started. Bulimia and binge eating disorder have a significantly lower risk of mortality than anorexia.

We began this section with an extremely important sentence. We make no apologies for repeating it: we hope you will repeat it to yourselves over and over again.

**People can and do recover from eating disorders.**

## My eating disorder

*I hate the words 'eating disorder'. When people use these words to describe a condition that you have, you feel exposed. People see you differently. A lot of people think they understand, but they don't. People trivialise it, label it and pass it off as young people trying to look like models. If only it were that simple. All I know is, when I look in the mirror I usually hate what I see. I hate what I look like and I see nothing but fat.*

*I am very conscious of what I eat, which causes many problems. Some days I don't feel hungry or want to eat at all. When I do eat I feel guilty a lot and worry about what I have done. You can never get away from it; it's just one challenge after the next. I envy people who don't think about the food they eat or who are happy with themselves the way they are. I would actually hate for anyone to go through what I do because it is very lonely and exhausting. I hope that one day I will be able to be happy with myself and enjoy eating, rather than dreading it.*

REBECCA, 16

*I often feel completely alone because I do not have anorexia or bulimia. I am not really thin, in fact I am overweight. My problem is that when I eat I can't stop. I eat and eat until I feel like my stomach is going to burst and then I just sit there and feel really low about everything. I look at myself and I hate what I see. I am going to counselling and I am trying to control it, but it's hard. Sometimes all I can think about is food. However, I am determined to get control of my life, I don't want the eating disorder to win and that is what keeps me positive.*

SIMONE, 15

*I want to get well, but I don't want to eat 'normally' either. I don't want to put on weight, but I don't want to be sick all of the time. I am constantly confused and tired. When it comes down to it I am beginning to get too tired to fight about eating and drinking any more. I am thinking more and more about what it would be like to simply surrender to 'healthy eating' and let go of my worries, fears and anxieties about food. Obviously that will not be an easy thing to do, but I am thinking about what it would be like which is a start. If I push myself a little more each day, I hope that eventually I will be strong enough to fight my eating disorder. I will also have my family to help me. They may never completely understand, but they love me.*

SHANNON, 17

*I was always a big child. I was not as small as the other boys in junior school and even at a young age that made me feel uncomfortable. When I was in senior school I remember getting very fixated on my appearance and experimenting with dieting to lose weight. I think my eating disorder developed from there. I just felt like I was never fit or thin enough. All of my energy went into my eating habits and exercise. Eventually I didn't really think about much else. It was my mum who first spoke to me with her concerns about how little I was eating and how much exercise I was doing. After that my girlfriend told me she was worried too. It's strange, because for a long time I felt like everyone else had a problem but me. I am so thankful to everyone who stood by me, especially my girlfriend. Recovery taught me so much about myself. I learned about the people I love, the person I am and how much I want to live and be happy. These are the things I am going to hang on to.*

PAUL, 19

*My parents helped me get through my bulimia. They loved and supported me during some difficult times. There were many times when I threw their love and support right back into their faces. I would reject them because I wanted to be left alone. I saw my body as my own and no business of theirs. Somewhere along the way I became friends with them again and saw that they were trying to look out for me. It did take me a long time to get there though. I feel bad for putting them through it, but I did not choose to have an eating disorder and I cannot change the past. I am now looking forward to going back to school and seeing more of my friends. Things will be different though as I will not have my bulimia to fall back on when things get tough. I need to cope on my own in better ways, but luckily my parents will be there to encourage and support me when I need them.*

LAURA, 18

# CHAPTER TWO

# How will the eating disorder affect you?

We hope that the information given so far is helping you to make more sense of your child's state of health and behaviour. The young people's accounts show that eating disorders must be taken seriously; they also emphasise the importance of parents as carers. Two features of the book that continue to appear throughout the following chapters are relevant quotations from parents and 'How can you help?' This chapter is about the effects of the eating disorder on you, your immediate family, relatives and friends.

## Desperate to help?

From the moment you suspect your child has an eating disorder you will be desperate to help, ready to try anything to make them well again. You might try any or all of these approaches: buy gifts in the hope that this will make them feel happier; smother them with time and attention to make them feel special; bribe them, giving in to unreasonable demands if they promise to get better; devise reward and punishment systems based on efforts at recovery; confront them and shout at them; try forcing them to eat.

> *I am not afraid to admit that I would have done just about anything to take away my daughter's bulimia. In the beginning I tried to make her feel good by treating her to shopping trips and buying her expensive gifts. We had fun, but it didn't change anything.* ROBYN

*At first, all I wanted to do was believe that if I just spent more time with my daughter and gave her more attention, she would be OK. I tried this. I gave up many things to be with her and centred most of my life on her. Unfortunately this does not work, as it is not about our relationship and I cannot control her illness.* KATE

Robyn and Kate are loving parents who sensed their daughters' unhappiness. Their own anxiety levels were high: action seemed essential. Robyn offered time and 'retail therapy'; they had a good time and probably forgot about the eating disorder for a few hours. Kate, who decided that more time and attention were needed, sacrificed important aspects of her own life to achieve this. Neither approach had any lasting impact on their daughters' eating disorders.

Many readers will understand what motivated these two parents and some of you will have had similar experiences. Treats and shared activities are an important part of normal family life but they will not make your child's illness disappear. Teenagers will sense parental desperation if bribes for recovery are offered, and play on it, but they cannot recover to order. Rewards and punishments seem an inappropriate way to set about encouraging recovery, and are likely to lead to future problems.

You know from the previous chapter that an eating disorder is a complex and potentially serious illness. You also know that your child is likely to recover but that recovery takes time. There is no quick fix that we know of, no magic wand, no miracle cure.

## HOW CAN YOU HELP?

- Offer normality and consistency, however strange life seems at the moment. Continue with your usual family routine, which probably includes spending time with your children, going on holiday, giving pocket money, funding hobbies and special interests and perhaps occasional surprise gifts. What matters is to avoid the temptation to make changes simply in the hope of making your child better.

- If your child is too unwell to enjoy previously enjoyed treats and activities, consider appropriate substitutes, but avoid giving them the impression that they are in any way being punished or rewarded for being ill.

- Seek outlets for your anxiety and frustration. Activities or interests of your own will absorb you and give you a break, even if only for a short time.

- This might be a good time to find out what help is available for parents. Some of the services offered by EDA include self-help groups, the adult helpline, online support through the website and the website message board. Investigate counselling possibilities in your area, too. It's important that you have some way of expressing your feelings and talking about your experiences and worries that is safe, confidential and unthreatening.

- Think about the things you can be doing, such as observing and noting any symptoms or changes, considering what you will say to the GP and how you will cope with your own emotions.

- Give your child enough space, in terms of time and opportunity, to take some responsibility for their eating disorder. You want them to become independent enough eventually to look after their own basic needs, physically and psychologically. If the eating disorder has made you realise that your children need more quality time and attention, by all means begin to address this, but not at the expense of their growth as individuals.

- Find our more about local treatment options and the NICE (National Institute for Health and Clinical Excellence) treatment guidelines (see Chapter Six).

## Coming to terms with your child's disorder

Once you accept that your child has an eating disorder, you are bound to wonder why this has happened. Parents often decide that it must be their fault, that they have failed their child in some way, as Susan does:

> *All I could do when I found out about my child's eating disorder was cry. I thought about all the things I could have done that might have caused it, I just wanted to make it all better for them.* SUSAN

It is easy to find fault with yourself since there is no such thing as a perfect parent. Susan seems to be searching for reasons to blame herself. Your child will probably make hurtful accusations, too, especially when the *voice* is speaking. If you think it's your fault you will feel guilty. This can trap you into vowing to make your child better. If you look back to the previous section you will understand how blame and guilt can lead to desperate efforts to help. It is not helpful or useful for you to take inappropriate blame for your child's eating disorder.

## HOW CAN YOU HELP?

● You want things to improve, but punishing yourself with blame, guilt and tears will not help towards the recovery process. Accept that your child has an eating disorder and give yourself permission to stop agonising over the past. Then you can put your energy and parental expertise into the present situation.

● Outside support can help you to do this. If this sounds daunting, begin by visiting the EDA website; then perhaps try calling the helpline.

● Personal support is also important. If you are on your own it is even more important that you set up some support for yourself as soon as possible. Even if there are two of you working together on this, you may both still benefit from talking openly to a trusted friend or relative. Try to choose someone who will not be judgemental or try to take over. Good support will boost your confidence and help you take a more balanced view of the eating disorder.

● Ask your child how you can help. They will probably be pleasantly surprised that you have asked and may have some good ideas that seem workable. Be wary of suggestions that you are not comfortable with, but be honest about your reservations.

● Be encouraged when your child wants to talk, especially if they have been reluctant to do so in the past. Remember that inability to cope with painful thoughts and feelings lies somewhere behind the disorder. When possible listen attentively at the time, but if you are about to go to work, for example, decide on a time when you can both get together and honour that arrangement. However, be prepared for their mood to have changed by then!

● Once your child feels safe to talk, there will be many more conversations, some with the child you know and probably some with the *voice*. You will be learning throughout this process and so will your child, even when you both seem to be going round in circles. This will be tiring and challenging; that's why you need support for yourself.

- Try to recall something positive that's happened each day, not necessarily connected with the eating disorder, and encourage your child to do the same. Keeping a diary can be therapeutic for you and your child. Many teenagers do this anyway.

- Continue your research into eating disorders, keeping a note of anything that seems useful.

An eating disorder is a serious illness. Your child did not choose to be ill: you want your child to get better. This will be a challenge for you all. You do not have time to waste on notions of fault, blame and guilt.

## Feeling frustrated?

However much you love your child, however hard you work to help with recovery, you will often feel extremely frustrated with their behaviour.

> *I can't tell you how many times I have had to go outside and count to ten when I have been around my eldest daughter. Her anorexia makes her ask endless amounts of questions about calories and meal times are very difficult. I know it is not her fault, it just gets to me sometimes.* MICHAEL

Michael reveals knowledge of the eating disorder and understanding of his daughter's very real anxiety but this doesn't make him superhuman. He tries to be patient but his frustration is hard to control. He uses a quick, simple but effective way to calm down in this situation and avoids losing his temper, but this is a constant drain on his energy. He is supporting his daughter practically and emotionally, but at a cost.

Mealtimes are a daily source of potential frustration but you will also experience the deeper frustration of wondering when or whether this illness will ever end, especially if your child doesn't seem to want recovery.

### HOW CAN YOU HELP?
- Remember, it is the eating disorder that has caused your child's behaviour to change. Michael was quite clear that this motivated his

daughter's obsessive questioning. He knew she wasn't setting out to annoy him.

● Like Michael, you will find ways to minimise difficult situations. Sometimes you will lose control, because you're tired and because you're human. You might be able to talk about this with your child when you're calmer.

● This example should help you see why support for parents is so important. Whether you manage to stay calm, as Michael does here, or occasionally lose control, you will find it helpful to talk about your frustration to someone who isn't directly involved. That way it will not be building up inside you.

● Devise your own strategies for releasing your more deeply felt frustration when it threatens to overwhelm you. You might shut yourself away to read, write, paint, watch a video or listen to music; gardening, going for a really brisk walk or cycle ride will suit others; practising yoga or meditation can help; you might have friends you can visit at short notice.

## Feeling confused?

Feelings of confusion are another inevitable effect for parents. Eating disorders are complicated illnesses, involving many contradictions. The whole experience will feel unreal, almost nightmarish at times, whatever stage you are at – wondering whether your fears are valid, plucking up courage to voice your concerns or trying to access treatment.

> *I found everything confusing from the beginning, but especially when it came to getting my child professional help. It felt like everyone was speaking a different language, and I was left to try and interpret what I could. This is hard, when the only thing you want to do is help.* RACHEL

Rachel could not understand the professionals at times: they were probably using technical terms that were unfamiliar to her and perhaps discussing aspects of treatment which they were involved with on a daily basis, but which were completely new to her. She struggled to make sense of it all and felt excluded because although she was present, no one explained things to her clearly. Rachel needed to know what treatment was being offered, why it was thought suitable and what it involved.

There is also the confusion that arises from differing views about eating disorders and treatment. This is inevitable with health issues, as fresh knowledge and expertise are acquired while established beliefs are questioned. Eating disorders are often featured in the media, but these usually focus on one or two individuals, whose case histories may be very different from your child's. Dramatic stories sell papers and magazines, attracting viewers and listeners; they might raise or dash hopes but they are unlikely to influence your child's rate of recovery. Newspapers are particularly prone to reporting small advances in existing treatment as if they are major breakthroughs, when in fact they will need many years of further development before they can be used on patients.

## HOW CAN YOU HELP?

- When you have an appointment with your GP or healthcare professional, make notes beforehand of your main concerns and any specific questions you want to ask. Highlight the most important points so you can make best use of the limited time available. If you have your notes and a pen ready as soon as you sit down, it will be obvious that you expect to contribute.

- Whenever terms are used that are new to you, ask if they can be explained. If you seem to be given conflicting advice or confusing information, say so. Even when everything seems clear, it's a good idea to check back briefly before you leave.

- If your child is involved in the consultation, the GP may want to talk to them alone for at least part of the time. In any case you should beware of talking over your child as this may make them feel their views and feelings don't matter or are being ignored.

- You will gradually gain confidence in your own grasp of the subject, but remember to make use of books, publications from EDA and the EDA website, where you will find a carers' message board. If you're feeling muddled and isolated, try the helpline.

## You and your partner

This is about you and your relationship with your partner.

> *The more ill my child became the less time I got to spend with my husband. Eventually the only thing we ever had any time for was a quick chance to talk about what bills needed to be paid and my son's eating disorder. We became two strangers living in the same house.* REBECCA

> *My daughter's eating disorder made it impossible for me to pursue my relationship with my boyfriend; there just wasn't any time. Everything I did was about how I could work it in with being there for her. I eventually felt so depressed, I felt like I no longer had a life of my own.* SHEILA

Rebecca and Sheila both speak with painful honesty about the loss of quality time with their partners. Rebecca and her husband spoke only of essential domestic business and, of course, the eating disorder. Sheila felt unable to spare time for her boyfriend but became depressed without that morale-boosting adult relationship.

Be honest with your partner about these difficulties rather than ignoring the problem. Let each other know that your relationship does still matter. If the suggestions below are not workable for you, devise an alternative. This may be particularly important if the partner you live with is not your child's parent or if you are in a relatively new relationship.

You and your partner will feel like strangers at times. Caring for a child with an eating disorder can drain you of time and energy. However, this is precisely why partners matter; you need that mutual support and you both deserve occasional distraction from the illness. The relationship needs care and protection if it is not to become a casualty of your child's eating disorder.

### HOW CAN YOU HELP?

- Make time together a priority, even if it is only an hour or two once a week. You may need to plan this and write it on the calendar. If necessary, take it in turns to decide how you will use this time. Be realistic so you don't waste the time you've set aside stuck in a traffic jam or arguing about which film to see. An hour in the local pub, coffee with good friends or a walk with the dog, any of these can help recharge the batteries that keep your relationship working.

⬤ Try to avoid talking about the eating disorder during planned time together, but be wary of making promises you might be unable to keep. Perhaps more important is to limit it to five minutes each to sound off and then to leave the subject for a later, specified time.

⬤ If this is new to you and you're thinking 'that's impossible', give it a try, even if at first neither of you can relax. Finding time for your partner is not a luxury; it's essential for your emotional health and self-esteem. As you become more used to spending some time together on a regular basis you may find that you return to your child feeling a little more positive.

⬤ You are also showing, by example, that relationships have to be worked at, that there is life outside the eating disorder and that leisure activities are important.

## Brothers and sisters

Many of you will have other children, the brothers and sisters of the child who is ill. These siblings, whatever their age, will sense that something is wrong. They will be aware of parental anxiety and tension: they will be aware that your attention is increasingly focused on one child, who may seem to be acting a little strangely. They will become very troubled if they do not understand why the atmosphere at home has changed.

> *Explaining to my seven year old son and twelve year old daughter that my eldest child had bulimia was the most difficult thing I have ever had to do. I thought long and hard about how I would go about it and I think the most difficult thing for me was trying to explain it to my seven year old who knew something was wrong, but didn't know what. Basically you need to do the best you can, and be honest. You may need to alter your language according to the age of your child to help with their understanding, but the basic principles are still the same. Be sensitive, approachable and honest with them. You will only make them less prepared for things to come if you keep them in the dark.*
> SAMANTHA

Samantha realised that she must explain things to her other two children, and thought carefully about the best way to approach each child. She prepared them for further changes, which helped to give them confidence in her ability to cope.

## HOW CAN YOU HELP?

- Let the child who is ill know that you intend to be open with the other children. Eating disorders thrive on secrecy and the *voice* will not like this. If you have already promised not to tell, explain why you have changed your mind.

- Talk to your children. Tell them about the eating disorder as simply and honestly as possible. Encourage them to ask questions and do your best to answer them. You want them to feel free to talk and ask questions whenever they need to. Keeping them in the dark will create more problems, making them afraid and anxious.

- Be aware that younger siblings are likely to blame themselves; this unfounded guilt can make them extremely unhappy. Make sure that they are not being made to keep secrets or tell lies. They must know what to do if asked to hide, eat or buy food secretly. You might need to talk to the young sufferer about this, too.

- Remind all your children about the need to show affection and not alienate each other.

- You may have to cope with apparently conflicting requests to make of your children. You want them to behave normally and not worry unduly, but you also need to prepare them for difficult situations and issues, which may be far from normal.

- For teenage siblings, EDA has an award-winning booklet 'How can I help? Information for friends and relatives of someone with an eating disorder'. The EDA Youthline is there for young relatives and friends as well as sufferers.

When a brother or sister has an eating disorder, siblings might react in a number of ways which can include: becoming angry, even confrontational with their brother or sister; showing jealousy or resentment of the extra attention their brother or sister is getting; seeming as stressed and upset as you; competing with their brother or sister, in some way, to gain your attention; wanting to care for their brother or sister, even trying to take over from you; trying to avoid the issue altogether. These are understandable reactions to a strange, unsettling illness. Talking openly and listening respectfully will help. You will need to manage the situation on a long-term basis.

*It is very difficult when one child is very ill but you have two others to look after as well. You want to be able to spend time with all of them and make sure that they are all coping with what is happening, but you feel as though you have very little time and tend to put the needs of the child with the eating disorder first. You then feel guilty about the effect this must be having on the others.* LOUISA

Louisa, like Samantha, wants to care for the child who is ill but doesn't want the other children to feel neglected. Talking to them about this will not be enough. There will have to be compromises, perhaps, and new ways of coping with family life.

## HOW CAN YOU HELP?

- Encourage your children to continue with their hobbies and interests. Some will feel guilty about enjoying themselves when one child is ill and unhappy, unless you reassure them that the best way to help is by keeping themselves occupied and reasonably cheerful.

- Allow them to take part in after-school activities and to spend time with friends after school and at weekends, if this is what used to happen. Try to find time to have a chat when they return. They need to know that you're pleased to see them. If you're too tired or feeling tearful because of difficulties arising from the eating disorder, tell them and make time to catch up later when you can listen properly.

- Organise a simple family activity, perhaps once a week, that will be absorbing and fun. Suggest a ban on talk about the eating disorder on these occasions. Whether you're going to the coast, walking in the woods, playing a game or watching a film, remember that laughter is an excellent medicine. An eating disorder is a serious illness, but you do not want your children to lose their joy in life. None of you should be afraid to laugh. Laughter is free and can help release stress and tension.

- Try to arrange time with each child separately in addition to the family activity. This should be a time when they feel free to ask questions about the sibling who is ill but also to talk about their own concerns, which might be squabbles with their friends, the eating disorder, how things are going at school, saving the planet or why a pocket money increase is needed.

- Your children may have really good ideas about how to help. Listen to them, however impracticable their suggestions might seem: they need to feel valued. Sometimes they will look at problems more clearly than you.

- Encourage your children to express their feelings through drawings and writing and any other medium you think relevant.

- It is possible that family therapy might be suggested (see Chapter Six). This would involve all members of the family so perhaps now is a good time to think about how any brothers or sisters might feel about this. Family therapy will involve working together as a family with a therapist. The therapist specialises in encouraging communication without trying to blame anyone, and then working on ways the family can support each other in the future.

## Secrets and promises

We have encouraged you to voice your concerns to the child who has an eating disorder. You know how important it is that they acknowledge the problem; until they do there is little chance of recovery. In the previous section, about your other children, we emphasise the need to be open with them about their sibling's illness. Your children will talk to other people anyway and shouldn't have the burden of not telling placed upon them by anyone.

The more open you and your family are, the less frightening this illness will seem. Your child may resist this, especially if they experience the *voice*, which will be threatened by openness. You will have guessed already that secrecy is not appropriate, but we do understand the reasons why some parents try to keep their child's eating disorder a secret…

- You're afraid that people will think badly of you.

- You worry that people will treat your child differently once they know.

- You dread being given advice about how to *make them better*.

- You still want to pretend it's not really happening.

- You're embarrassed or ashamed that your child has an eating disorder.

- Your child has made you promise not to tell anyone else.

These all seem powerful reasons for keeping the eating disorder a secret, as this mother knows:

> *Before my child developed their disorder, we were a very sociable family and would regularly meet up with relatives and friends. Everything changed when she became ill and I started to retreat away from social interaction for fear that people would see our family differently. I was also scared that if people found out, they would blame her father and me for her disorder. This scared me, so we kept it a secret for a very long time.* SAMANTHA

Samantha allowed her daughter's eating disorder to disrupt her social life, because she was so afraid of other people's reactions. Perhaps she feared their reactions because she and her partner believed it was their fault. Avoiding relatives and friends probably caused needless misunderstanding and confusion for everyone. Samantha must have run out of excuses at times; she and her husband lost a valuable social life when they most needed it; they became increasingly cut off from normality; the eating disorder and all its complications continued.

> *Every time we were invited to attend a family event, my daughter would either refuse to go or hide away from everyone to avoid being forced to eat or asked questions. Eventually people began to notice that something was wrong and started to ask me questions. I didn't know what to say as I didn't want to betray my daughter and I didn't want anyone judging her or us. Even close loved ones can be judgemental at times. I just made up more and more excuses which again made things worse.* CAROL

Carol's problems arose from her daughter's distress at social functions. When asked about it herself, she felt unable to answer, partly because she was afraid they would both be judged unkindly. There is another factor here, though, as Carol uses the phrase 'betray my daughter', which suggests that she had promised her daughter that she wouldn't tell anyone the truth. Again, this parent ended up in a web of deceit.

### HOW CAN YOU HELP?

- Discuss the implications of secrecy with your partner. If you cannot agree, work towards a compromise, but we would urge you to be open with your closest relatives and friends.

- You should not be constrained from doing this by your child. Tell them what you're intending to do, by all means. The eating disorder affects you and you have a right to let people know, especially those who care about you and your family.

● If you have made promises to your child not to tell, say that you are sorry but you made a rushed decision under pressure, which you now regret and explain why. Offer to let them know when you are likely to tell someone else.

● Decide who to tell first; the others will be easier. Try to remember that this is an illness, not a crime. The calmer and more matter of fact you can be, the better, but if you are clearly upset a good friend or relative will offer you a tissue and make a cup of tea. Better still, some might offer to help in the future. If they really mean it, accept and tell them what would really be helpful.

● Be constantly wary of secrets and promises while you are living with an eating disorder. Both can lead to lies, deceit and needless loss of trust.

## Relatives and friends

These people may have been worried already, perhaps noticing changes in your child's appearance or behaviour. Some might have guessed at the cause; others will have no idea. The EDA helplines are often contacted by close relatives, such as grandparents, who are concerned about someone in the family. Certainly you will be asked questions and so will your child. Taking the initiative, by telling those closest to you as soon as possible, should take the pressure off everyone in this respect. Be ready for a variety of reactions:

● Some will listen without being judgemental, show concern for your family and offer to help. These people will be invaluable as support for you in the future, so accept their offer and keep in touch. You can ask them straight away to avoid making comments about appearance, weight or the amount of food eaten. This should make it easier for your child to cope with social gatherings.

● Others will betray their ignorance of eating disorders by making unhelpful suggestions or tactless remarks. You must decide if these people are worth the time and energy needed to explain in more detail.

If they are making you feel bad or unsettling your child, you may choose to avoid them when possible.

● Be careful with anyone who thinks they know *just how to sort it out.*

● Bear in mind that one or two might have such massive worries of their own that they are unable to concentrate on your situation.

● Relatives and friends are welcome to ring the EDA adult helpline for information and for suggestions about supporting you and your child. There is a useful EDA booklet, 'Understanding Eating Disorders', which they can ask for. Tell them about the EDA website where there is a huge amount of information available.

## A sense of normality

Of course family life will be different, at times seeming abnormal, unreal and sometimes a nightmare, according to the state and severity of your child's eating disorder. Normal family routines are often changed and disrupted to meet the needs of the young sufferer.

*Our lives got turned upside down when our daughter developed her disorder. We did everything we could to get her well and often that left very little time for anything else. You can't just fit the illness into your schedule. It becomes a big part of your life.* KAREN

Karen's description illustrates the eating disorder's capacity to overwhelm a whole family. This also undermines everyone's confidence in each other and eventually everyone's health suffers.

*As soon as I realised how severe my daughter's problem was, I became completely fixated on making her well again. I lost a lot of friends because I simply made no effort with them any more. For a long time I became a complete recluse and felt as if I was living only to care for my daughter. I had this idea that one day she would get better and then I could have my life back again.* JENNIFER

### HOW CAN YOU HELP?

● Keep to your old domestic routines as far as possible, including meals, shopping and basic care of children and pets. Bedtime is especially important for children, whether it involves frequent nagging about time and a half-hearted kiss from a teenager, or a story and cuddle with a younger child. Checking that homework is done in the evening and getting everyone off to school the next morning are things that still matter and ensure that life is not put on hold.

- Try making a list of chores and leisure activities that you undertake as individuals and as a family. Work out which are essential, which can be dropped and which might still be possible by using your family resources differently. Involve the family in a discussion of these matters; you might be surprised by offers of help with specific chores and some original suggestions on adapting to a new normality.

- Think carefully and talk to your partner or a trusted friend before making any dramatic changes to your life, such as giving up work and cancelling social events, holidays, courses, club memberships and enjoyable activities. The eating disorder may be around for a long time but eventually your child is likely to recover. You and your family are vital to that recovery process, but putting your life on hold will not hurry it up. You need some pleasures in your life in order to be strong enough to cope, even if at the worst times you are unable to enjoy them as before.

- However, this is probably not a good time for unnecessary upheaval, such as moving house or changing schools, in the hope that such changes will help recovery.

There were suggestions in earlier sections about finding time for your partner and your children. If there are friends and relatives who are keen to support you, perhaps they can help you to manage this.

This is about maintaining a sense of normality by taking some control back from the eating disorder. It's about looking after everyone's health as well as taking extra care of the child who is ill with an eating disorder. Young sufferers are prone to guilt about the trouble they are causing their parents and siblings: a sense of normality will reassure them that they haven't ruined family life completely.

## Sharing the responsibility

As parents you have responsibility for your children, but when one child is ill with an eating disorder you will feel that responsibility even more keenly than usual. You may be tempted to take on all the care yourself, even if your partner or others wish to be involved; you may be feeling resentful that you seem to be doing everything, running yourself ragged while your partner's life seems barely affected.

Another related issue concerns your child's ability to manipulate parents emotionally, which Laura's experience typifies:

> *I feel that my partner and I did not communicate as effectively as possible about what was going on and that made it very easy for our daughter to manipulate situations in order to get what she wanted. She would ask me if she could walk the dog when she was already weak from exercise and I would say no for fear of her collapsing. She would then talk to her father and tell him that I had said to ask him. He would occasionally say yes and that would cause her father and I to have huge arguments.* LAURA

Young sufferers are driven hard by the eating disorder: they will seek to divide and rule where two or more parental figures are involved in their care, whether or not they live in the same house. Laura's daughter wanted exercise, knew her mother would not allow it but guessed rightly that she could persuade her father otherwise, resulting in unsafe exercise and a row between the parents.

### HOW CAN YOU HELP?

- Your child needs consistency of approach, especially from parents. Teenagers can be ruthless in getting what they want; eating disorders can cause them to be devious and manipulative. They may lie, as Laura's daughter did, not understanding the consequences.

- This means that you must discuss your general approach, but also keep each other informed when new issues crop up. Your child is likely to lie at times and will try to drive a wedge between you and your partner, so check with each other when discrepancies arise.

- Think about the balance of your roles. Try to avoid one parent being the tough disciplinarian all the time while the other is the gentle carer.

- If there are two of you in the home, aim to support and encourage each other. Gently remind each other of what else is going on in your lives and in the outside world. It might be worth catching the news, on radio or television, during the evening at a time when you can be together. Sometimes this will put your own difficulties into perspective, if only for an hour or two.

- Try to have a catching-up time with each other once a week, semi-formally, when you can review any changes in approach you have agreed on and look ahead to the following week, so you can share out basic chores and extras, such as GP appointments or parents' evenings at school.

- If there is no other adult living with you, you must get some practical help as well as emotional support from relatives and friends. This will mean telling them about the eating disorder and letting your child know what you're doing. Asking for help is not easy, but those who care about you and your child will be pleased to be asked, and you need it to survive.

- If you really feel there is no such person, you might contact your local council or social services about your eligibility for carer breaks or respite care. Your local library will have information about organisations that might be useful, and so would any nearby branch of Citizens Advice Bureau. There are a number of organisations for carers on the internet.

- EDA has some self-help groups for carers which offer mutual support; there is also a section of the EDA website dedicated to carers.

# CHAPTER THREE

# Caring for your child

For many readers this will be perceived as the key chapter because of its special relevance to you as parents. If you have read from the beginning of the book, you will not be surprised to discover that even here the first section is concerned with your needs. Although there are references to food-related issues in most chapters, including this one, we have devoted Chapter Four exclusively to this crucial aspect of caring for your child.

## Caring for yourself

You must take care of yourself if you are to remain strong enough to be able to care for your child to the best of your ability.

> *I was completely focused on caring for my child and did not ever give a second thought to myself. I thought that thinking of myself would be completely selfish, even though at times I really felt so tired that I thought I would collapse. My child needed me and I could not just ignore that. Occasionally I would feel depressed and wish I had a little more of a life, but then I would always feel guilty about it and focus on being there for my daughter. It was a very difficult situation.* CAMERON

Notice how Cameron thought it would be 'completely selfish' to think of himself and even felt guilty if he ever dared wish for more of a life. Yet this selflessness brought him to the point of collapse through sheer exhaustion.

*I went through a phase where I blamed myself for my daughter's eating disorder. You run through in your mind all of the reasons why this has happened and often you feel like one of them. It makes you feel like a failure. You need to get past these feelings and concentrate on what is really important. For me, that was supporting my child and trying to be positive. It's healthier for everyone.* KELLY

Kelly did not look after herself at first, because she continued to wear herself out mentally and emotionally. You can sense the relief she felt once she focused her energy on 'what is really important' and realised that being positive was better for everyone.

## HOW CAN YOU HELP?

- Accept that you may never fully understand why your child has been affected by an eating disorder. If you can stop asking your child 'Why?' perhaps you can stop asking yourself and persuade others to do the same. Explain that you want to focus on recovery. If this issue still bothers you, talk to your GP, your child's specialist or someone else who has some understanding of the issues, such as an EDA helpline worker.

- If necessary, have a list of simple tasks to tackle any time you find yourself going down the blame route, phone a friend or find time for a chat about other matters with your child.

- Understand that looking after yourself is not selfish. Being a carer is physically and emotionally tiring and unless you replenish those energies you will become less effective in your care role.

- You matter as an individual in your own right, not just as a carer. Try to set aside an hour or two for yourself each week, an opportunity to make use of any offers of help you've received. Use this time to make yourself feel good, whether you're reading in peace, listening to your choice of music, having your hair cut, going swimming, gardening or getting in touch with friends. It might even be a long, leisurely bath. What matters is that the rest of the family respect *time out* especially if it has to be taken at home.

- As time for yourself becomes more acceptable, perhaps you will feel less guilty about it. Eventually you might even look forward to *your* time.

When you return to the hard work of caring for your child, you should feel calmer and better able to cope.

● It is also important that your child sees you looking after yourself by making time for some privacy and relaxation. They need to understand that looking after yourself is a responsibility, not a luxury.

● Do remember to seek out and make use of support for parents. You can use the EDA helpline or the website to access information about a range of support, including counsellors, self-help groups and contacts, and the carers' message board. Talking through issues with others can be a very helpful coping mechanism, again something you would ideally like your child to do.

● Think about seeing your GP on your own account if you are really struggling.

● There are a number of organisations with information about grants and support available for carers in the Appendix at the back of the book, including the Department for Work and Pensions.

## Talking about the eating disorder

You may feel that it is difficult to talk to your child since they developed an eating disorder. You are scared of saying something wrong or unintentionally making the problem worse. Young people in the grip of an eating disorder can often be very sensitive and quick to take offence; temper tantrums are a common characteristic of an eating disorder.

> *I was so terrified of approaching my son about his bulimia that I kept putting it off and putting it off. I didn't want to make matters worse and I was scared he might take something I said the wrong way and resent me for it.* IAN

Ian's fear of upsetting his son delayed that first vital approach which we discussed in Chapter One. While his son's bulimia became more entrenched, Ian continued to worry about his son's health yet the thought of speaking about it became more daunting with every day that passed.

*I felt like I was walking on egg shells all of the time around my daughter. I tried to rely on my wife to do all of the talking with her, but that wasn't fair. I did say things the wrong way sometimes, but I always managed to work it out with my daughter in the end. What's important is that you continue to try and never give up. You can't worry too much either about every single word you say. You never know what is the right thing to say, so just give it your best.*

THOMAS

Thomas talks of 'walking on egg shells', a phrase we frequently hear from parents who call the helpline. He wanted to be involved and he persevered, taking time to resolve misunderstandings with his daughter. Because he refused to be frightened off by difficult conversations, he became confident enough to stop agonising over every word.

## HOW CAN YOU HELP?

- You must not be so afraid of upsetting your child that you avoid talking to them, whether you are trying to pluck up the courage to voice your concerns for the first time, dealing with issues that arise on a daily basis as the illness progresses or offering support during recovery.

- If you have to broach a really difficult subject directly connected with the eating disorder, think about it first, talk it over with someone else if possible and then jot down your main points. Decide how you'll begin, but avoid trying to script your conversation beyond this or you could end up sounding insincere and unable to think on your feet in response to what your child has to say.

- During a more casual conversation try to avoid unnecessary comments on appearance, weight or food. This is particularly important during mealtimes at home and at social events involving meals or food. You might need to explain this to your family and friends.

- Open questions along the lines of 'How are you feeling?' or 'How has your day been?' can be interpreted freely and the response may give valuable insight into your child's current concerns. They are not threatening or judgemental in themselves, whereas closed questions such as 'What did you eat for lunch?' or 'Have you just made yourself sick?', which sound confrontational, are more likely to be ignored or dishonestly answered.

- You will often want to burst out with comments like 'But that's because you're so thin!' or 'If you ate less and did some exercise you'd feel better!'. Such remarks may relieve your frustration at the time but they will have no impact on the illness and might result in greater efforts to avoid engaging with you.

- When you do talk, try to listen patiently to your child's views, however distorted and illogical they seem to you. Agree to disagree over contentious issues or talk of different perceptions rather than trying to label opposing views as right or wrong. The more you can retain mutual respect and trust, the more likely it is that your child will meet you halfway in your efforts to communicate.

- Keep your wits about you: be wary of secrets and promises, as discussed in Chapter Two.

- Remember the way recovery takes place in stages as described in Chapter One and bear in mind which stage you think your child has reached. This will affect the way they talk, especially if they're in two minds.

- If your child experiences the *voice* learn to recognise it. It's OK to challenge the views of the *voice* but this may be difficult if there is no logic behind it, so try not to make it a confrontational issue. In time your child should be able to question the *voice* as well.

## Education

Your child's education is likely to be affected by their illness: appointments and treatment sessions will sometimes occur during school hours and ill health may cause frequent or prolonged absence. Teachers may realise that something is wrong when a student's personality alters without explanation. School friends can become so worried that they seek out a trusted member of staff or call our confidential Youthline for guidance.

> *The school kept calling me and each time I would get a panic attack and put them off again and again. I didn't want to betray my daughter's trust by telling them about her eating disorder but I was worried that if I did not say something soon, the situation would get worse.* BETH

Beth had fallen into the trap of promising not to tell anyone at her daughter's school, yet knew she should keep the staff informed. This conflict was compounded every time there was a call from the school. If you are in Beth's situation, now is the time to tell your child that you have to break the promise because keeping it is making things worse.

## HOW CAN YOU HELP?

- Take the initiative if possible. Once you believe your child has an eating disorder, inform the school anyway, even if your child seems well enough to attend full time. The more you and the school co-operate, the better the chances of recovery. You will be able to offer mutual support and information as well. Your child may be angry about this at first, but if their education matters to them, there may be relief later that there is no longer a need for pretence.

- Notify the school on the first day of absence. If you forget, or there is an emergency and you run out of time, ring the next day and explain.

- Remember that absence without notification is seen as 'unauthorised absence' after ten days. When unauthorised absence occurs, an Education Welfare Officer or an Education Social Worker will be asked to find out why your child has been absent. It is their duty to do this and their main concern will be to ensure that your child's education continues.

- If you become really concerned that prolonged absence is affecting progress and morale, contact the school and ask about services for children too ill to attend. Home tuition may be available.

- Progress towards recovery is subject to setbacks and will not comply with external deadlines. You must be clear in your mind what your priorities are, in order to support and reassure your child if health issues have to take precedence temporarily over academic achievement.

- For many young sufferers, there is pressure to perform well and fear of letting people down at all stages in their education. Pressure can come from teachers, parents and friends, but the greatest pressure often arises from sufferers' own high standards and expectations. This is one of the many issues you will have to talk about.

● Achieving high grades in exams may become less important if it means your child becoming too ill to go to university or start work.

## Employment

If you are in paid employment you are likely to experience difficulties over requests for time off and increased absence from work.

> *I was so secretive about my son's anorexia that I kept making different excuses to my boss about why I needed time off. Eventually, my boss asked me what was really going on and I had no choice but to tell them. I feared the worst, but they were actually quite good about the whole thing. It felt good to be honest and consequently my boss allowed me to work more flexibly, which has really helped.* ROBERT

Robert describes a scenario now familiar to readers of this book: secrecy often makes matters worse. His boss didn't understand what was going on and fortunately took the initiative by raising the subject with Robert. The outcome was positive for all concerned but this situation could have led to unpleasantness and even more anxiety.

### HOW CAN YOU HELP?

● Take the initiative by asking to speak to your employer as soon as you know your child is unwell. At least you will have tested the reaction and you may find your honesty is appreciated. You could offer the EDA helpline number, information leaflets or website address if your employer wants to know more about eating disorders. You could also ask for this to remain confidential if that is what you prefer.

● If you do need time off work because of the eating disorder, check your contract of employment to be sure of your rights.

● If unsure or in case of difficulties with your employer, seek advice. The following organisations can help: Citizens Advice Bureau, Advisory Consultation and Arbitration Service and the Department of Trade and Industry. Contact details are given at the back of the book, including website addresses.

● If your child is in employment this section will be relevant to them, too. This will be a difficult issue to discuss, but one that will have to be tackled.

We hope you are beginning to understand why we have emphasised the importance of looking after yourself.

## Boundaries and behaviour

This is really quite simple: your child needs boundaries.

You may prefer the word *rules* but what we are talking about here is the need to set limits on how far a young sufferer can push behaviour before you say 'No! That's not acceptable, however ill you are.' Every family and every society has a behaviour code of some kind to ensure the safety and survival of the individual and the group.

Your difficulty as parents is that healthy teenagers seem programmed to test rules. They frequently choose to be *out of bounds*, which may affect how they dress, attitudes towards school, what time they come home on a Saturday night, how they speak to you and other more troubling issues.

You have the additional problems that arise from an eating disorder. Some of you may long for 'normal' teenage behaviour problems, as some young sufferers can seem docile and almost too eager to please authority figures. This compliance can change when the young person is affected by an eating disorder that they are desperate to maintain.

> *I know that I have to understand that when my daughter is enraged with anger and lashing out at me that it is not her, it is her eating disorder, but it really hurts. I try to be supportive and caring, but when she says that she hates me, I wonder if what I am doing is really helping. I am not going to give up though, my daughter is very important to me.* MEGAN

Megan conveys poignantly the pain caused by her daughter's cruel remarks, yet many readers will have had similar experiences with children who do not have an eating disorder. This parent tries to remind herself that it is the eating disorder at work, but worries that she may be failing as a carer. She does not give up on her daughter, though, and perhaps knows that her daughter may be in a very different mood the next day.

## HOW CAN YOU HELP?

- You will already have a set of family boundaries or rules. These can still apply, as long as they are not obviously damaging to your child, such as a compulsive eater being expected to prepare family meals or put away the week's food shopping. You may need to discuss such anomalies with your children, so that reasons for exceptions are understood.

- You know your child, and the changes in behaviour that arrived with the eating disorder. Direct observation of your child, combined with the information you gain from reading, will enable you to work out what is acceptable because of the eating disorder and what is not. Forcing siblings to eat food they don't want is unacceptable; leaving the toilet or bathroom in an unpleasant state is unacceptable; opting out of a big family celebration might be understandable and acceptable. Such situations need calm thought and discussion, but eventually a decision must be made.

- An experienced eating disorders professional once said 'Rudeness is not a symptom of anorexia'. It might be useful to remind yourself of this observation from time to time. It can be applied to all eating disorders.

- If you refer back to Chapter One you might connect the concept of the *voice* with some of the behaviour problems you encounter. If you think of this as the extreme version of your child's negative state of mind, you might choose to discuss specific boundaries when you feel the positive state of mind is in charge. Mealtimes are dealt with in the next chapter, but a poor time to discuss this issue is either just before or during a meal, when anxiety levels will be highest. At a better time, your child may have useful suggestions to make.

- Whenever possible, try to separate your child from the behaviour caused by the eating disorder, so it is clear that you dislike the behaviour, not your child.

- You will sometimes have to explain that their behaviour is upsetting siblings. They need help to cope in a different way, rather than being made to feel bad as a person.

The next five sections concern behaviour that can be particularly difficult for parents to deal with.

## Excessive exercise

Young people in the grip of an eating disorder can become obsessive about exercise, especially if they are suffering from anorexia or bulimia. You may notice a steady increase in the duration, frequency, variety and level of exercise undertaken. This is excessive exercise and it is potentially dangerous when combined with decreasing calorie intake and continued weight loss.

> *When my daughter first started exercising a lot, I thought it was just a phase. It wasn't too long before I realised it was out of control. She was very thin, but even at an extremely low weight, she would want to exercise. I had to get very strict with her about the amount of exercise she could do. She did not like me for this at all.* TAMARA

Tamara initially dismissed her daughter's excessive exercise as 'a phase', not understanding that the eating disorder was thriving on it. Her daughter's physical weakness did not deter her at all: she was driven by the desire to burn calories and stay thin. Eventually Tamara's anxiety and common sense prevailed and boundaries were set. She had to endure her daughter's anger and there were probably some very unpleasant scenes over this.

Young sufferers are ingenious at finding many ways to exercise, some more obvious than others, such as:

- committing themselves to additional sports activities at school

- taking to extremes or distorting advice from athletics coaches and dance teachers

- jogging, cycling, walking the dog for miles, swimming for hours, attending several aerobics sessions a day

- offering to help with domestic activities such as cleaning the house, shopping or gardening

- running up and down the stairs many times, standing rather than sitting, tapping their feet, tensing their muscles, secretly exercising in their room, even setting the alarm clock so they can do sit ups in the night

## HOW CAN YOU HELP?

- Raise concerns early on, as soon as you begin to feel anxious. Avoid accusations, but show concern, asking what they think. With older children, there are limits to what you can do, but at least talk about the long-term dangers of what they are doing.

- Be clear in your mind what matters most: your child's health must take priority over your dread of their reaction.

- Your child will be very upset if much-loved activities have to stop and they will also be really worried about weight gain. Remember this if they defy you later. Remind them that you have a right to know what they're doing and a duty to protect them from unnecessary harm. This is when you might need to consider alternative activities that will give pleasure or distraction.

- If you are confident about your decisions, you may find your child willing to co-operate later, perhaps even helping to draw up an exercise regime that is acceptable to you. You should be able to get advice on what is appropriate from the school nurse, your GP or the practice nurse.

- If your child is involved in sport or dance at a fairly competitive level, try to speak to the professionals they work with. Dance teachers and athletics coaches sometimes call the helpline to talk about such worries. There are books and publications about sport, dance and excessive exercise.

- Be aware that excessive exercise can cause many health problems, including slower metabolism, muscle soreness, bone injuries or fractures, headaches, loss of co-ordination, recurrent illness, apathy and concentration problems.

We realise that for some of you this section will be frustrating if in fact you are desperately trying to encourage your child to do some exercise. Since there is widespread media coverage about problems of obesity in young people, those who exercise to excess will often use such news items to suit their own agenda.

## Rituals and routines

You may notice strict rituals and routines developing. These are time-consuming and exhausting for the sufferer, intensely irritating and puzzling to the observer. Your child might:

- always eat from one special plate

- cut food into tiny pieces

- follow rigid meal times

- wait five minutes between every mouthful of food eaten

- check the calorie content on every packet of food

- clean their bedroom thoroughly every day

- shower several times a day

- wash their hands repeatedly in scalding water

- hoard worthless objects

- perform chores in a set order, starting all over again if they make a mistake

- check over and over again that they have locked the door

> *My daughter has many obsessive behaviours. They are very difficult to manage and we often struggle to decide on what is and isn't OK. All we want is for her to have a happy and healthy life.* JANICE

Janice touches on boundaries here, in talking of 'what is and isn't OK'. She also refers to 'obsessive behaviours'. There is a condition known as Obsessive Compulsive Disorder (OCD), which might be identified if the rituals and routines we list above escalate to such an extent that your child's life is really limited by this behaviour.

### HOW CAN I HELP?

- Be aware that such behaviour seems absolutely necessary to your child. It gives a sense of security, however false, and lessens anxiety temporarily. While these rituals and routines are being followed, the sufferer doesn't have to think about anything else. It is therefore really important that you treat this behaviour as part of their illness and avoid notions of accusation, blame and punishment.

- Many of our examples involve food and eating. This can be a direct effect of semi-starvation: prisoners on limited food rations do the same things. If you think about this, and remember that anorexic sufferers are denying their hunger, these particular rituals may seem more understandable. Many of us will try to make a special meal or edible treat last as long as possible.

- Another explanation for food-related rituals is the great anxiety young sufferers will experience at mealtimes, when the prospect of eating food they do not want is terrifying. For others the fear is that there will not be enough food – ever. Perhaps for all eating disorder sufferers there is the underlying fear that if they start to eat they will never be able to stop.

- You do have the right to decide which rituals and routines you are prepared to live with and which you are unable to accept. This is another example of the need for boundaries. The way to decide is to consider the effect upon you and the rest of the family. So the insistence on a particular plate doesn't hurt anyone else, but expecting the whole family to eat at a particular time might not be possible. If excessive showers are depriving others of hot water, that obsession will have to be curbed (in any case it may result in dry, unhealthy skin). You should not be accepting any demands that will cause needless financial hardship.

- If you decide that certain behaviours are unacceptable because of the effect on others, explain this and see if there are ways to lessen the anxiety this decision causes your child.

- If you suspect OCD make an appointment to see your GP and contact OCD Action or other relevant organisations listed in the Appendix at the back of this book. Making brief dated notes can help in such situations, so you are clear about the reasons for your concern.

- NICE (National Institute of Health and Clinical Excellence) have published treatment guidelines for OCD. Contact details are in the Appendix at the end of the book.

## Deceitful behaviour

Parents who call the EDA helpline often talk of the excellent open relationship they have always had with their child, who would never lie to them. It is hard for parents to accept, but eating disorders are so powerful that your child's previous honesty will be compromised by this illness: however much they love you, they are likely to be deceitful in order to maintain the eating disorder. The deceit can take several forms:

- Your child may use emotional blackmail, perhaps promising to give up the eating disorder if you end a relationship they disapprove of. Emotional blackmail may also be used to get what they want, by promising to give up bingeing if you buy them a Playstation or IPod, or threatening to lock themselves in their room if you don't buy more laxatives. This is a form of bullying: you may feel so desperate that you are tempted to give in to such demands. This will not make your child better and you may feel worse if you cave in. Eating disorders seek to control everyone and parents are vulnerable.

- Your child may lie, even if they have never done so in the past. Try not to take this personally: this is about survival, survival of the eating disorder. There may be lies about what the GP said, lies about eating at a friend's house, lies about weight, lies about the inpatient unit and lies about what you or your partner has said. Do not assume that everything you are told is a lie, but do assume that some of what you are told is not true.

- Your child may seek to deceive you and professionals by artificially increasing their weight just before an appointment, by drinking lots of water, putting stones in their pockets or hem, or wearing heavy jewellery, footwear and clothes. They may hide food, steal money and try to bribe siblings to cover up for them.

- They will become expert at trying to play off one family member against another, especially parents who live apart.

*My son would often lie about the amount of food he had eaten, how much exercise he was involved in and how much he weighed. It just got to a stage where I thought he was lying about everything. I wanted to trust him, but I felt as though I couldn't. The trust comes back though slowly, as they get better.*
JENNIFER

Jennifer must have found her son's habitual lying frustrating and upsetting. The worst effect of this is that trust can be so eroded that parents never believe what they're told. It is reassuring to note that as her son recovered and felt less threatened by the eating disorder, Jennifer regained her trust in him.

## HOW CAN YOU HELP?

- Avoid compounding the deceit by pretending to be taken in by it. Explain your doubts and explain that you understand why there is deceit, but make it clear that you would prefer honesty. If, for example, money goes missing, you must say something. Try to make it easy for your child to come clean without too much loss of face.

- It is particularly important that siblings are not blamed for 'crimes' they have not committed: this will cause terrible resentment. Similarly, remember to check with your partner about what each of you has said before assuming that your child's statements are either true or untrue.

- Take care to avoid pressuring your child into dishonesty by trying to extract impossible promises from them. If you are planning a family holiday and your child has been refusing to eat carbohydrates and fats for months, asking for a promise to eat normally while you're away is as unfair as it is unrealistic.

## Self-harm

Some eating disorder sufferers will also self-harm; many will not. It is upsetting for parents to discover that their child is deliberately inflicting pain by cutting, burning and hitting their own body. It can be hard to accept if, like Charlie, you are not prepared for it:

*I first noticed that my son was self- harming when I saw loads of tiny cut marks down the inside of his arm one day. I asked him about them and he said that it had happened during an accident when he fell from his bike onto the road. I thought this was a bit odd, but I didn't ever imagine that he would lie about such a thing so I thought no more of it. About two weeks later I noticed that they were there again. Now I was worried, but I thought maybe he was being bullied at school. I never would have thought that he had done it to himself. It has been really tough to see him going through all of this, but I am determined to be a good father and help him get better, no matter how long it takes.* CHARLIE

The deceit we discussed above is illustrated here: Charlie knew the bike story didn't ring true but let it go, which suited his son, as the cutting made him feel better. Self-harm appears to offer:

- release or escape from painful emotions, including disgust at having an eating disorder

- punishment for *being bad* which might include lying to you or having eaten too much

- cleansing, which might be physical or psychological in its effect, and perhaps gives a temporary sense of peace and self-acceptance

## HOW CAN YOU HELP?

- Find out as much as possible about self-harm, if this is affecting your child. We can only touch on this complex issue here. There are books and leaflets on the subject and we include contact details of the National Self-Harm Network at the back of this book. NICE (National Institute for Health and Clinical Excellence) has also published treatment guidelines for self-harm.

- If you notice signs of self-harm, mention them to your child. If you show calm concern rather than shock, it will be easier for you both to talk about it. You could give them the EDA Youthline number and of course you can talk about your feelings on the adult helpline or look for support on the carers' message board, which you can find on the EDA website.

- It might be easier for you both to focus on practicalities first: check that injuries are being cared for properly and ask how you can offer comfort when it happens.

- Boundaries might be necessary: your child may not be able to stop this but you have every right to insist that siblings should not see it happening (although self-harm is usually a very private activity) and to establish basic health and hygiene rules.

- Self-harm is extremely unlikely to indicate suicidal feelings or a wish to hurt others.

● If your child wants to stop, you might be able to help with distractions when the urge to self- harm is strong, by going out for a walk, playing a board game or watching a favourite video. Writing and drawing can be outlets for emotional distress, but don't forget talking.

● There are safer alternatives to self-harm such as pinging themselves with an elastic band.

## Mood swings and depression

We use the phrase 'mood swings' for sudden, unpredictable and dramatic changes from one mood or emotion to another: from joy to despair, from happiness to fury, from sadness to fear.

Seasoned parents of teenage children may think that this is nothing new, but with an eating disorder the severity of the sufferer's moods and the speed of mood changes can leave carers exhausted and confused. Most of the issues covered in this chapter will be complicated by your child's emotional state. We talked earlier of the two minds, the two contradictory ways of thinking your child will reveal at different times: each state of mind will evoke different emotions, too. Your child's ability to think clearly can be affected by severe hunger and poor nutrition. Any apparent threat to the eating disorder is a major disaster and the emotional fall-out affects those closest.

> *I found it hard to deal with my child's mood swings. I knew that they were a result of her eating disorder but sometimes she would fly into uncontrollable bursts of anger which were usually directed at me, and that's hard not to take personally. She would then feel very guilty afterwards and fall into a depression about her behaviour. What do you do when this sort of thing is happening to your daughter? How do you help them when you are the one they are lashing out at?* CATHERINE

Catherine's daughter experienced three moods in quick succession: anger, guilt and finally depression. There is logic in the sequence but we don't know what triggered the initial 'uncontrollable' anger, which must have been frightening for both of them. There are no tried and tested answers to Catherine's anguished questions, except that probably you have to be mentally prepared for these destructive moods and in quieter times talk with your partner and your child about ways of handling them.

Catherine describes the third mood as 'a depression'. Low self-esteem is at the root of most eating disorders and depression will often be experienced alongside the disorder. This is not a passing, temporary, emotion but a serious mental health illness that will have to be addressed.

## HOW CAN YOU HELP?

- Recognise triggers for mood swings and aim to minimise their effect. Situations involving eating are looked at in the next chapter, but there will be other highly charged situations. Talk with your partner, your child if they're willing and anyone prepared to act as a sounding board to help you devise damage-limitation strategies to try next time.

- The calmer you are the better but that will sometimes be impossible. You could try to imagine that you are wearing a flak jacket designed to resist emotional fallout. You might recall attempts to contain your child's tantrums as a toddler, for there are similarities.

- After a particularly difficult mood has passed, you could both write about it and then share your different perceptions of what happened and how it felt to you. This might be an opportunity for you both to discuss the power of the *voice* (see Chapter One).

- You and your child both need someone else (perhaps a health professional) you can talk to openly and honestly about difficult moods and mood swings.

- You may need to look at boundaries with your child, especially if siblings are suffering as a result of these alarming outbursts of anger. Be clear that it is the behaviour that you have a problem with, not the person; say what is not acceptable and explain why.

- If your child is showing signs of serious depression, talk to your GP and keep a note of any remarks and behaviour that particularly worry you. If your child is older, encourage them to make an appointment on their own behalf. There are many self-help and information books about coping with depression. You may also find that you need information and support if your own health begins to be affected by a deeply entrenched eating disorder in your child.

# CHAPTER FOUR

# Food, eating and mealtimes

Since this book is about eating disorders, the topics in this chapter are particularly significant for parents who are caring for young sufferers. You have to think about food every day with extra sensitivity, whether your child is ill but in denial, undergoing treatment while living at home or working hard to recover. If your child is an inpatient you will have to prepare yourself for their return and if your child is away at university you have the holidays to cope with. We have kept this chapter short and the headings simple for ease of reference, but we do not advise you to turn to it in the midst of a chaotic mealtime.

If you are reading the whole book straight through you will notice that there is some repetition in the self-help chapters. This is partly because some readers will only dip into specific chapters and partly because key underlying themes are relevant throughout. You may be irritated by some of our suggestions in the 'How can you help?' sections as they are so much more difficult to put into practice than to present as theory. Remember that there are other books to turn to; by now you will also be working out your own ways of coping with your child and your particular situation.

## Food

We eat to stay alive, we eat to live healthily and many of us socialise by sharing food with others. Yet food can become the new four-letter word when your family is affected by an eating disorder. To your child, food is the enemy.

> *I don't know what to do about feeding my daughter. She says she will only eat salad with no dressing or dairy products, but when I prepare it there always seems to be something wrong with it. I then worry for hours after she eats that she might be throwing up her food anyway. It's so hard to know what to do. I just want her to be OK. I have no control, I feel helpless.* CAROL

Carol and her daughter are both being controlled by the eating disorder. The food described here consists mostly of water, hardly any calories and very little nutritional content, but even that might not be eaten and, if it is, Carol worries that her daughter will get rid of it later.

## HOW CAN YOU HELP?

- Dramatic and distressing scenes involving food will occur. Use what you learn from these episodes combined with some forward planning to help reduce their severity and frequency.

- Most parents try to provide nourishing, appealing meals although their children will not always eat the 'right' amount or variety of food. Unless told otherwise by a healthcare professional, there is no point in trying to force a child of any age to eat food they really dislike. Recall early days as a parent when you first offered solid food: wasn't it often spat out or simply refused? You couldn't force it down but you continued to offer food.

- Remember that none of us can enjoy food when we are upset. Your child is likely to dread meals and other occasions when food is on offer: fear, mistrust and anger do not aid digestion. We consider mealtimes later.

- Accept that if food is eaten only to please parents or to get mealtimes over, it is likely that purging will follow. If your child is older or living away from home, you will have little influence over their food intake anyway.

- Check relevant nutritional facts: what a good balanced diet should include and the recommended calorie intake for your child's build and age. Ask for information at your medical practice. You must be confident if you are to counteract the *voice*, which will be loudest at mealtimes and whenever food is discussed. Treatment might include a structured eating plan drawn up by a healthcare professional.

- Involve your child in choices about the food you provide, but make the boundaries clear; so you might offer choice about which protein food to add to the salad, but you don't offer to exclude protein.

- Ask your child to write down foods that are still, in theory, enjoyable or at least bearable. With some input and boundaries from you, perhaps you could compile a compromise list of possible food purchases and meal ideas.

- If wholesome food is eaten without too much fuss, don't worry if the same food is asked for several days running. You can negotiate variety later. Offering a similar amount of food at each meal might be helpful, too.

- Sufferers who consistently undereat may express preferences for strong flavourings such as chillies or sharp pickles. This is a sign of semi-starvation rather than a desire to eat. As with sudden demands for sweets or junk food, which can be encouraging to parents when little else is being eaten, these foods are very limited nutritionally.

- Vegetarianism isn't necessarily a problem but do check out details with The Vegetarian Society for yourself. Many people with an eating disorder use vegetarianism as an excuse not to eat the food normally available, possibly because their understanding is distorted by the *voice*. This can also apply to any other information about food that your child acquires.

- Resist requests to join slimming clubs, or to follow commercial or magazine-inspired diets: these are not safe ways to regulate food intake for a young person for whom food is such a distorted issue.

- Binge food can be a problem and requires sensitivity and firmness. You will not be able to ban bingeing but you can insist that there's enough cereal and toast for everyone the next morning, that siblings' Easter eggs are not eaten and that some food is *out of bounds*. They should not steal food from others. You might want to store out of the way foods you used to have freely available, but think carefully about the impact of this on siblings.

● It is most important that the sufferer sees you and your family enjoying food and eating normal helpings.

## Cooking

This heading covers any food preparation, whether it's beans on toast or a three-course celebration meal. We will also mention shopping for food in this section.

Some young sufferers prefer to have food shopping and preparation taken out of their hands completely: that way they feel less responsible for what they eat and therefore less guilty. As long as you are happy there is no problem with this, although when recovery seems more likely you might want to encourage a bit more involvement in this basic skill for independent living in the future.

Others are keen, perhaps too keen, to take over food shopping and cooking for the family: they get pleasure from being around food and like being in control of what others eat. This is not a good idea.

> *I thought it might encourage my daughter to eat if I allowed her to cook for the family. Like most things at first it was fine, but before I knew it she was being very demanding about how much we had to eat and it seemed as though the portions she was giving us kept getting bigger and bigger. It seemed wrong to say no to her cooking for us, but I knew that things were getting out of control.*
> MARK

Mark's initial thinking seems logical, but it didn't work that way, as he discovered. It is likely that as his daughter piled on food for the family, she was eating less and less herself. Although Mark realised that things were getting out of control, he found it difficult to address the issue as his daughter seemed so happy to help.

### HOW CAN YOU HELP?

● Politely but firmly turn down offers of help with shopping and cooking for the family, if you believe your child has an eating disorder. Explain that this is not appropriate while food is such a serious issue. You could suggest help with washing up or other household chores instead.

● You might consider allowing a *cook for yourself only* approach. Older children will be doing this, especially if they live away. If it is your kitchen and you are paying for the food, do be ready to make boundaries clear.

● If you are already in a situation like Mark's, you may have to make yourself unpopular by removing the privilege of cooking for the family. Explain why but don't expect to be understood! The *voice* will not like the loss of control.

● When you are cooking for your child, you may be tempted to cheat by reducing or increasing a meal's calorie content. The temptation is understandable but be aware that if you're caught out there will be a serious loss of trust. Cooking favourite meals or leaving edible treats in the fridge is unlikely to tempt the entrenched young sufferer if eating has become severely restrictive, whereas for the binge eater this will be too hard to resist.

● Honour any agreements made about cooking and serving food. This might involve a set amount served on a special plate. If the special plate is breakable, consider having an identical spare ready to avoid needless distress if the original gets broken.

## Eating

For most of us, eating is both a necessity and a pleasure, but for the young person with disordered eating the act of consuming food is perceived as torture inflicted by heartless parents. Binge eaters and compulsive eaters punish themselves, rarely enjoying the taste of the food they consume and hating themselves for it later. Young sufferers can hold strong beliefs about eating:

*I don't deserve to eat*

*I will get fatter after only a mouthful*

*If I start eating, I won't be able to stop*

*If I put on any weight I am a failure*

*If I put on weight nobody will love me*

*Not eating is the only thing I'm good at*

These beliefs are hard to challenge because they are not based on logical thinking. Food has become muddled up with feelings; the young sufferer's fragile self-esteem is at risk with every mouthful eaten. Devious efforts to avoid eating will be made such as:

● cutting food into tiny pieces, then pushing them around the plate

● hiding food in pockets or sleeves

● dropping food under the table for pets to eat

● sliding food onto siblings' plates

The longer the eating disorder persists, the smarter the sufferer gets at pretending to eat. If eating is unavoidable, compensatory action such as purging or exercise will be taken as soon as possible to prevent weight gain.

> *You cannot watch every single move your child makes 24 hours a day 7 days a week. It's just not possible. Even when you are watching them you know that there is a chance that you might miss something anyway. I have caught my daughter out many times now stuffing food into her clothes as we ate, when she thought I wasn't watching. The problem is that she gets better and better at hiding these things* KAREN

You probably have to accept that sometimes less is eaten than you think. Karen eventually realised that she could not watch her daughter all the time she was eating. Most of us would hate to be watched closely as every mouthful is eaten; if you are still eating together you have to pay attention to the rest of your family. You need to eat, too!

## HOW CAN YOU HELP?

● Remember that the anxiety about eating is real. For most this is caused by fear of weight gain: even a couple of ounces will seem disastrous. Others dread the temporary sensation of bloating that is often experienced and some find food so disgusting that eating it makes them feel contaminated as it enters their body.

● Ask your child about these feelings, but not while they are struggling to eat. Let them know that you're noticing attempts to hide food, as an observation rather than an accusation. Your awareness and understanding should help your child to relax a little and perhaps gradually feel less anxious.

- Try working out an eating plan with your child, a few simple rules that you can agree on to make eating less stressful. This might involve time, place, company, what is offered, how much, how it's cooked and presented. A routine can help everyone cope more confidently.

- When your child begins to eat a little more healthily, recognise how much they have achieved and offer praise if you think this will be appreciated, but avoid commenting on weight gain.

- You may have to ensure they do not rush off to the toilet to purge after eating.

## Mealtimes

If your child has an eating disorder, mealtimes are likely to be challenging, however hard you try. Strategies suggested above should help you all to manage mealtimes acceptably but you will have to accept that sometimes they will be disastrous. Even the more civilised meals may be dominated by obsessive questioning about calories and fat content.

*Mealtimes were the best part of some family's days, not ours. Meals were emotionally draining and incredibly hard. I actually began to dread them. My son literally could not control himself around food. He became a different person. He would talk about the fat content in everything I put on the table and how 'disgusting' it all was. It made it difficult for me to eat my food.*
JAKE

This is another family that is being controlled by the eating disorder. You might have to talk to everyone normally present at mealtimes; find out what each family member finds really unacceptable and what is putting them off their food. This is what had happened to Jake, whose dread before meals was often justified by his son's subsequent behaviour. Jake was unable to enjoy his food and other family members must have felt the same.

## HOW CAN YOU HELP?

- The longer you can manage everyone having meals together, if that was your old mealtime custom, the better; this helps give a sense of normality. If this is too miserable for all concerned then work out an alternative approach, but make this decision away from mealtimes and let everyone know what's been decided and why.

- Ask the child who is ill how you can be supportive during meals without causing distress to the others. Be clear about what you can agree to, such as allowing them to take as long as they need, but letting the other children leave the table when they've finished.

- You might suggest that there is a ban on talk about the eating disorder during mealtimes: you won't nag about what your child is eating, but in return you don't want to hear questions about calories.

- However stilted the conversation might be, try making mealtimes a social event in that each person has an opportunity to talk about the day and what's been upsetting, funny or interesting.

- Having music playing, as long as it's acceptable to everyone, might help.

- You may have to let your child eat alone if the eating disorder is deeply entrenched or if it involves eating habits such as 'chew and spit', which will be too much for other family members to cope with.

## Food and the family

As you and your family learn to manage the eating disorder, you will find yourselves questioning some of your attitudes towards food, which plays such a vital role in your lives and has emotional significance way beyond its basic function.

Many of us try out weight loss diets because we are dissatisfied with our appearance and bore our friends with talk of 'being bad' or 'good' in connection with what we've eaten. We use food as a reward or consolation and it is often given as a present. We joke about our own bodies and sometimes we are unkind about other people's appearance. There is a tendency in our society to judge people by their looks and dress, rather than on personality, characteristics, talents and skills.

*After my child developed binge eating disorder, I realised just how strong a person's emotional link with food can be. It also caused me to look at myself and my other children's relationship with food and our bodies, and although we thought it was harmless, we would often joke about being 'fat' or feeling bad for eating junk food. I didn't ever realise I was doing it. It's something everyone does from time to time. For example, I can't count how many times I must have said, 'Do I look fat in this outfit'? I was told by a specialist to avoid such comments, as they can often be a negative influence on a person who is affected by an eating disorder.* CAROLYN

Carolyn is very honest about the way she and her family had used food and appearance as a common source of jokes and self-deprecating remarks. You are bound to notice similar patterns in your family and you will wonder if these had an impact on your child. You may be able to promote a more positive attitude within your family as a result of your experiences and newly acquired awareness of these issues.

## HOW CAN YOU HELP?

- When you notice yourself starting the 'Do I look fat?' routine you could make a point of changing it to something like 'Do you think this colour suits me?'.

- Avoid making jokes about other people's appearance, body image, weight or diet and challenge your children and partner when they do this. Keep it light, so you don't make them feel guilty and explain why you've been thinking about this.

- Look for rewards and ways to celebrate that do not involve food, but don't apologise for enjoying food or for having the occasional second helping.

- You might like to discuss *mouth hunger* where you long for or crave the taste of certain (usually high fat or high sugar content) foods versus *stomach hunger* that comes from a need to take in more nourishment.

- Make a point of complimenting your children on their helpfulness, skills and achievements, so they build up their self-esteem by valuing themselves more for who they are rather than what they look like. This can be applied to partners, too.

# CHAPTER FIVE

# What are eating disorders?

This is a brief introduction to the medical aspects of an eating disorder. For more depth and detail look for specialist books on this complex subject: there is an extensive booklist on the EDA website. We describe briefly the signs and symptoms of specific eating disorders; we also touch on the serious long-term effects. This information may come as a shock to readers who are new to the subject; unfortunately it is unlikely to deter young people entrenched in an eating disorder. If you have had an eating disorder yourself, or if you are still in recovery, you may find this chapter quite painful to read.

## Who develops an eating disorder?

Anyone can develop an eating disorder, regardless of age, gender, cultural or ethnic background. Those most likely to be affected are young people aged between fourteen and twenty-five. However, it is not uncommon for adults to develop an eating disorder much later in life or for an eating disorder that began in adolescence to persist for decades. Cases have been reported of children as young as eight years old developing anorexia. It is estimated that approximately 10% of known sufferers are male, but this could be as high as 20%.

Research suggests that over one million people could be affected by an eating disorder in the UK. However, only a small percentage of them have been diagnosed and are receiving appropriate treatment.

## Common features of eating disorders

An eating disorder is a serious illness that affects the physical and psychological health of the sufferer. Food is used in some way to control or block out difficult thoughts and feelings. Stress, depression, sadness and low self-esteem may be too painful to bear, especially for a young person. Eating disordered behaviour seems to take away the pain.

Eating disorders do not usually result from a single cause. They are more likely to be the result of a complex mix of factors such as traumatic experiences, unpleasant emotions, unrealistic expectations and perfectionism. For many sufferers the eating disorder appears to give back control over their lives but the longer the illness persists, the more likely it is that the eating disorder will be in control.

Having an eating disorder can cause shame and even despair. To cope with these feelings, some people will self-harm or misuse substances such as alcohol or drugs. Sufferers often struggle on their own to overcome their eating disorder and related problems. They are unlikely to succeed and their failure can make them feel even worse about themselves.

## What are the warning signs?

As with any illness, a note of caution is needed here: many of the warning signs mentioned in this section have little significance on their own but you may have cause for concern if you have noticed several of them, especially if they are increasingly obvious.

Please bear in mind that some of these signs can also be observed in perfectly happy, healthy teenagers! In the following sections we give more detailed information about specific eating disorders.

The desire to be thin or to be less heavy is a sign that may be only too apparent in some cases, but in others it will only be revealed in what is said: there may be an obsession with body shape and size; constant fascination with food, calories, weight and the connection between these three; increasingly rigid views about what food is 'good' or 'bad'; apparent guilt about eating and sometimes a tendency to compete with others to be thinner and to eat less. Significant weight loss may be hidden by baggy clothing; this can also be worn by those who are overweight or believe themselves to be so.

The desire to change body shape and weight makes normal eating a problem; sufferers are clever at finding ways to avoid eating, restricting the amount and variety of food consumed or concealing what is being eaten. Meals may be skipped and only small portions will be eaten when eating is unavoidable. Food must be low in calories and fat, becoming vegetarian or vegan can be hijacked in order to refuse previously acceptable food, while chewing gum and diet drinks may be used to suppress the appetite. Unwanted food might be hidden in the bedroom; the fridge or food cupboards may be raided secretly. Empty food packaging may be left lying around, as if the sufferer wants to be challenged.

Many excuses will be given for not eating, but sometimes disordered eating affects the family more directly. Eating in front of others may be avoided whenever possible, meals may be expected at set times or else refused and, more surprisingly, sufferers may try to buy and cook food for others which they will not eat themselves.

Other warning signs involve compensatory action taken when guilt is felt for what has been eaten: sufferers may disappear to the toilet to purge, exercise immediately after meals, use appetite suppressants or take laxatives. Many will exercise excessively and compulsively, perhaps taking suggestions from ballet teachers or athletics coaches to extremes.

## What is anorexia nervosa?

Anorexia nervosa means *loss of appetite for nervous reasons* but the extreme weight loss that is a major symptom of this eating disorder is achieved by denial of hunger rather than real loss of appetite.

Those who suffer from anorexia usually restrict the amount they eat and drink, sometimes to a dangerously low level, in order to lose weight. Their desire is to be thin. Excessive exercise can become compulsive for the same reason. Sufferers feel in control and therefore able to cope with life. Unfortunately, as the disorder progresses, they will become seriously underweight and are likely to suffer from malnutrition. The chemical changes in the body affect the brain and distort thinking, making it almost impossible to make rational decisions about food independently.

## Physical and psychological signs of anorexia

The most well-known and easily observed physical sign of anorexia is extreme weight loss, but poor or inadequate weight gain in relation to growth can also be significant. Sufferers experience circulation problems: because they feel cold even in warm surroundings they may need their baggy clothing to compensate for this and sometimes a layer of fine white downy hair is grown as the body seeks to protect itself. Distressing visible effects include dry, rough or discoloured skin, dull lifeless hair and bloating of the stomach along with a puffy face and ankles. Abdominal pains indicate constipation; dizzy spells and feeling faint are other unpleasant physical signs of anorexia. There are other less easily detected physical signs in female sufferers, including periods stopping or the delayed onset of menstruation. Hormonal imbalances can result in a loss of interest in sex, which can affect male and female sufferers. These hormone imbalances will lead to the development of osteoporosis (thinning bones), which also affects both sexes.

Intense fear of gaining weight is the dominating psychological sign of anorexia. It is accompanied by a distorted perception of body shape and size, and often encouraged by a powerful inner *voice* that challenges and controls the sufferer's food intake and exercise. There is usually an intense interest in what others are eating but an absolute denial that there is a problem, which is particularly frustrating for anxious parents. Personality changes and mood swings are often experienced: these can be far more extreme and unpredictable than normal teenage moodiness.

## Behavioural signs of anorexia

Apart from the very difficult moods mentioned above, the most obvious behavioural change involves rigid or obsessive eating habits, such as cutting food into tiny pieces and perhaps refusing to eat in front of anyone except close family members. Many layers of loose, baggy clothing serve the dual function of hiding weight loss and keeping the sufferer warm. Vomiting straight after meals or increasing use of laxatives are signs of anorexia that some parents are not aware of initially, assuming this to relate to bulimia only. Excessive exercise at the gym, at home or at school is a common sign of anorexia: the aim is to prevent weight gain at the very least and sometimes to induce further weight loss. You are likely to witness restlessness and hyperactivity along with the roller-coaster emotions, a combination which makes the sufferer's reluctance to talk about these signs of illness all the more difficult to cope with.

### Long-term effects of anorexia and recovery

The long-term effects of anorexia on the mind and body can be severe. Women who have suffered from anorexia can have difficulty conceiving and may eventually become infertile. As mentioned above, for men and women there is a high chance of developing osteoporosis or brittle bones. Heart and kidney problems are also common in long-term anorexia. Fortunately, for both sexes, many of the effects of the disorder can be reduced or reversed, once the body has received proper, regular nourishment.

Once recovery begins, it can take time for the body and mind to readjust. Because anorexia tends to reduce the amount of food the stomach can cope with, starting to eat and drink regularly again can lead to discomfort and feeling bloated. Bloating and weight gain are alarming prospects for the anorexic sufferer. Depending on the emotional difficulties the individual may be facing, mood swings and personality changes can take a long time to settle. For many sufferers the unrealistic expectations of family and friends can increase anxiety about the recovery process, which will be extremely stressful anyway.

## What is bulimia nervosa?

Bulimia nervosa means *hunger of an ox for nervous reasons,* but this can be misleading as some bulimic sufferers may eat very little at times.

Those who suffer from bulimia will consume large amounts of food at one time: this is known as binge eating or bingeing. This behaviour seems to block out or control painful thoughts and feelings. After bingeing, sufferers usually feel guilty and ashamed about the food they have eaten and look for ways to escape these feelings by preventing weight gain. Vomiting, taking laxatives or exercising excessively may be used to achieve this. As with anorexia, someone with bulimia may see the prevention of weight gain as a means of gaining control.

Bulimia is harder to recognise than anorexia, as sufferers often manage to maintain a relatively normal, healthy weight. For this reason the disorder can remain undetected for a long time, sometimes even years. Sufferers of bulimia turn to food to cope with low self-esteem and feelings of inadequacy. They are usually obsessed with their weight. Sometimes bulimia can stem from a belief that the disorder will be successful in preventing weight gain, where diets have failed in the past. Some develop bulimia after suffering from anorexia in the past.

## Bingeing

The term 'binge' is used to describe an episode of excessive, non-stop eating; these binges might occur several times a day, a few times a week or every day for months. There can be many variations in the frequency, timing and duration of the binges, which can occur quite separately from meals. Usually the longer a person has bulimia, the more reliant they become on these binge eating episodes. Binges often consist of foods that are high in fat or carbohydrates and are therefore high in calories. In extreme cases, a person may resort to eating strange foodstuffs such as dry pasta, condiments, partially defrosted frozen foods and even previously discarded food retrieved from the waste bin. The amount of food a person will consume during a binge will differ from person to person, but it can involve vast quantities and thousands of calories.

## Physical and psychological signs of bulimia

There is no single physical sign that gives a clear indication of bulimia on its own. Although some sufferers will become very thin, many will fluctuate in weight frequently while others will maintain a steady weight. Those who vomit are likely to complain of a sore throat and hoarseness, experience tooth decay and have bad breath. You may notice that the face seems to be more rounded; this is caused by swollen salivary glands. Skin and hair will probably be in poor condition and there may be hair loss. As with anorexia, female sufferers may have irregular or absent periods. Both sexes are likely to experience lethargy, tiredness and loss of sex drive. In time there is the possibility of problems affecting the heart and other internal organs.

The uncontrollable urge to eat vast amounts of food is probably the most obvious psychological sign of bulimia. Obsessive thinking about food will reveal itself in conversation, yet sufferers can be afraid to be around food because it makes them feel out of control. As with anorexia there is often a distorted perception of body weight and shape. Sufferers of bulimia often present a happy front to the world but they usually feel deeply unhappy, experiencing strong emotions and erratic mood swings. They may endure extreme anxiety, depression, low self-esteem, shame and guilt. Away from others they may feel isolated and helpless.

## Behavioural signs of bulimia

The irresistible urge to binge causes most of the behavioural signs of bulimia, although the binge eating sessions tend to occur when the sufferer is alone and able to binge secretly. What can be observed, or at least deduced by observation, is a range of behaviours aimed at getting rid of what's been eaten or compensating for it: disappearing to the toilet straight after meals to regurgitate what's just been eaten, frequent vomiting or increased use of laxatives, sometimes excessive exercise to prevent weight gain and periods of fasting. There is often great reluctance to attend social events that involve food. At home other family members may realise that food is disappearing unexpectedly or being hoarded. Large amounts of money can be spent on food, usually of high calorific value and low nutritional value. Sometimes money for food is 'borrowed' from others without permission and very occasionally the sufferer resorts to shoplifting for food. In some cases yo-yo dieting alternates with bingeing.

## Long-term effects of bulimia

The prolonged cycle of bingeing and then purging, by vomiting or using laxatives, can cause a significant loss of body fluids, leading to dehydration. Dangerously low levels of essential minerals in the body can affect the working of vital internal organs, sometimes fatally. Malnourishment can occur if the sufferer eats chaotically, missing meals or eating very little in between binge episodes.

Other potential dangers over a long period of time include damage to the oesophagus, rupture of the stomach, choking, erosion of tooth enamel, difficulty with swallowing and drying up of the salivary glands. Laxative abuse can lead to very serious bowel problems. Polycystic Ovary Syndrome (PCOS) is a condition that can affect women with bulimia. It can cause the growth of body hair, disrupt a normal menstrual cycle and affect fertility. PCOS can be treated using hormones.

As with anorexia, many of the harmful physical effects of bulimia can be reversed when the body is properly nourished.

## What is Binge Eating Disorder?

Binge Eating Disorder (BED) was only acknowledged as an eating disorder in its own right a few years ago. As with bulimia, sufferers of BED will consume large amounts of food at a time in an attempt to cope with difficult feelings and emotions. The earlier section on binges is equally relevant here. The essential difference between the two disorders is that sufferers of BED do not purge or take any other measures to prevent weight gain. If the disorder persists, steady weight gain is inevitable; this can eventually develop into obesity. Obesity carries the risk of further serious health problems, including high blood pressure, heart disease and a general lack of fitness. The binge eater is likely to become extremely unhappy with the weight gain, its effect on their health and their inability to control their eating.

Signs of BED include eating much more rapidly than usual, eating until uncomfortably full and eating large amounts of food when not physically hungry. Sufferers will often choose to eat alone, embarrassed to let others see how much is being consumed. Because they are also self-conscious about their weight, they often withdraw socially; if an event is unavoidable they will eat very little in public. They may often try new diets but soon become disheartened. Feelings of shame, depression and guilt follow episodes of bingeing: these feelings are likely to persist as weight is gained.

## What is compulsive overeating?

Compulsive overeating sounds self-explanatory but can be difficult for the non-professional to differentiate from binge eating disorder. Compulsive overeaters will eat frequently when they are not hungry, often knowing that they do not need, want or enjoy the food. At planned meals they may also eat far more than they need. There can be many variations of compulsive eating, but for many sufferers this behaviour happens every day for much of the day, especially when they are alone at home. For some the overeating comes and goes in cycles: eating might be relatively normal for days, weeks or months.

Sufferers tend to be overweight and feel great shame about not being able to control their need to eat. It is common for overeaters to hide behind a jolly façade and give the impression that everything is fine. Others, however, will avoid social interaction because they feel so unhappy with their weight and appearance. These effects of overeating may also provide a reason to avoid situations and events that they find difficult anyway. Compulsive overeaters are likely to suffer from obesity if this disorder persists.

## Atypical eating disorders or 'eating disorder not otherwise specified' (EDNOS)

Many people find that they are diagnosed as having an atypical eating disorder or EDNOS. This means that they may have some but not all of the symptoms of anorexia, bulimia, or binge eating disorder, or their symptoms may overlap two or more different disorders. In reality, the majority of all eating disorders are to some extent atypical or EDNOS. These disorders are no less severe nor will their impact on the sufferer or their carers be any less worrying. Atypical eating disorders or EDNOS should be taken seriously: professional help and support should be sought as soon as possible. Sufferers will normally be treated for the disorder that most resembles theirs.

Sometimes a diagnosis of 'partial syndrome' eating disorder will be made, if, for example, a woman with anorexia has irregular or recurring periods, or perhaps bulimic episodes are very infrequent.

## Other disorders associated with eating

Some eating problems are much more distinct, such as 'chew and spit' behaviour, when the sufferer chews normal or even large amounts of food and spits it out, rather than swallowing. Another example is regurgitation, when food is swallowed then brought back up into the mouth for re-chewing. Some people eat non-foods, such as paper tissues, to fill themselves up without the calorific intake. All of these behaviours are more common than many people believe and sometimes exist alongside other eating disorder symptoms. They can often be overcome with professional help.

## Prader Willi Syndrome (PWS)

This is not an eating disorder as such, in the sense that it does not have its roots in emotional problems. It's a genetic disorder that results in excessive eating from early childhood. People with Prader Willi Syndrome may not achieve full height growth, they may be prone to frequent temper tantrums and often have learning difficulties, all of which require specialist healthcare treatment and support.

## Pica

This is a disorder where people eat things which contain no nutrition. These might include dirt, stones, hair, faeces, lead, plastic, pencil erasers, paper, coal, chalk and wood. Pica most commonly affects children, but it also affects people with developmental disabilities. Pica may be unusual but is not always dangerous; nevertheless it may result in accidental poisoning or the accumulation of inedible material in the gut. Because pica may have serious medical consequences you should talk to your doctor about any worries you may have.

## Orthorexia

This nervosa is a term coined by Dr S. Bratman in his book 'Health Food Junkies – Orthorexia Nervosa' to describe the outcome of compulsive dietary behaviour based on eating only certain 'health' foods. It is not currently a recognised medical term.

# Related problems

Eating disorders carry with them many related problems that affect sufferers' behaviour, as well as their physical and psychological state of health. Ideally these problems should be treated at the same time as the eating disorder, but sometimes specialists may be unwilling to treat the eating disorder until the other issues have been tackled. Some of these related problems include:

**Substance abuse**, notably involving alcohol and drugs, offers another way for sufferers to deal with difficult emotions: these substances can help boost confidence and mood temporarily, and reduce appetite. However, physical and psychological health will be affected eventually, compounding

– and sometimes masking – the problems caused by the eating disorder. In cases of serious misuse, rehabilitation may be necessary before treatment for the eating disorder can begin effectively.

**Laxatives** are intended for the relief of constipation. They are available in many forms including tablets, syrups, granules and chocolate. Laxative misuse occurs when the user takes them frequently for a prolonged period or takes more than the recommended dose each time. The more often laxatives are used, the less effective they become, so there is a tendency to keep increasing the amount taken. Some eating disorder sufferers may misuse laxatives as they believe that doing so may help them to lose weight. However, most of the calories eaten are absorbed by the small intestine directly after eating, so using laxatives to prevent weight gain is not effective. Laxative misuse can lead to abdominal pain, bloating, dehydration, haemorrhoids (piles), irritable bowel syndrome, ulceration of the bowel, gastric bleeding and gastric ulceration, as well as depleting essential minerals such as potassium.

**Self-harm** is the deliberate injuring of oneself, often by cutting or burning. Other forms of self-harm include kicking or hitting a hard object, pulling hair out, biting and scratching. Self-harm is another way of coping with deep emotional distress, giving the sufferer instant relief and release. It can be very disturbing for everyone concerned, including close friends and family. It is important to know that self-harm does not mean that those affected are likely to hurt other people. It is a deeply personal way of expressing emotional pain and low self worth; self-harm should not be interpreted as a sign of suicidal tendencies.

**Obsessive-compulsive tendencies** may develop in some people who suffer from eating disorders. They usually become obsessed with food and calories, reading and absorbing every scrap of information available, becoming experts on nutrition, insisting on buying food and cooking meals for the rest of the family. In this way they get to be around food, but do not have to suffer the guilt of eating it. Exercise is another area where sufferers have a tendency to become obsessed, keeping to rigid routines and feeling agitated if unable to complete the level, amount or frequency of exercise they believe is necessary. They may indulge in excessive constant rituals: washing hands, cleaning, checking the light switch and other quite ordinary actions may have to be repeated compulsively many times. These behaviours are a way of controlling anxiety; however irrational and distressing they seem to the observer, they are very difficult to overcome.

**Depression** is very common in people who develop eating disorders. Symptoms include low self-esteem, sadness, exhaustion, being negative about oneself, the future and life in general. Other problems include disturbed sleep patterns, lethargy, poor concentration and loss of sex drive. Antidepressants can be effective in treating depression. However, other forms of treatment such as counselling or psychotherapy may be recommended. Sometimes a combination of medication and therapy might be offered. However, there are growing concerns about prescribing antidepressants to young people and there should be a very particular reason for them to be prescribed as they can have serious side effects.

**Mood swings** are a frequently experienced symptom amongst people of all ages in the grip of an eating disorder. The sufferer can seem completely fine one moment and then suddenly be overcome by bursts of tearfulness, anxiety, anger and depression the next. This can be confusing and worrying for family and friends, but also for the person concerned, who may not know what is causing these unpredictable moods. Do remember that mood swings are also a feature of normal teenage behaviour and do not necessarily indicate that your child has an eating disorder.

**Difficult behaviour.** Eating disorders can have a dramatic impact on a person's behaviour. Someone who has always been very open and truthful may become deceitful and secretive, perhaps lying about the amount of food they are eating, the amount of exercise they are doing or money that has disappeared. There may be attempts to manipulate others emotionally, especially parents, who are seen to pose a threat to the eating disorder, which the sufferer is desperate to protect.

**Dental problems.** People with anorexia or bulimia may experience some problems with their teeth, due to acid erosion of the surface of the teeth. Stomach acid washing over the teeth wears away the enamel layer of the tooth. This may lead to the pulp and nerve endings becoming exposed and the teeth may then have to be crowned or coated. Unfortunately much of the repair work undertaken to preserve the teeth of a person with an eating disorder will be ineffective unless they stop using self-induced vomiting as a method of weight control.

Drinking low calorie fizzy drinks, some sport and energy drinks or fruit based drinks can also have similar effects because of the acid they contain. Constantly sipping these drinks can be particularly harmful to tooth enamel.

Scrubbing teeth immediately after being sick is not advisable as this will damage the surface crystals on the enamel layer of the teeth. Dentists who specialise in problems related to enamel erosion advise rinsing the mouth thoroughly with milk, water or an inexpensive mouthwash containing fluoride. After being sick using toothpaste should be avoided; it is better to use just a toothbrush dipped in water.

# CHAPTER SIX

# Treatment and care

Here we consider important aspects of professional treatment and care, along with its implications for you and your child. Some of you may have turned to this chapter immediately; perhaps you bought this book already convinced that your child has an eating disorder. However, if you have not yet voiced your concerns at home, do read Chapter One so that you are aware of what might be going on in your child's mind. Eating disorders rarely go away of their own accord so professional input will be needed, but the prospect of outside help can be terrifying to a young sufferer.

## Making a start

It is a good idea to seek expert advice from a healthcare professional as soon as you believe that your child has an eating disorder. For most of you, the obvious place to begin is your local surgery or medical practice, where you and your family are registered with a family doctor or general practitioner (GP). There are some familiar faces, an environment you know and an appointment system that you are used to. Your GP is the front-line National Health Service (NHS) professional who knows your child, can make a diagnosis and initiate any subsequent referrals to specialists. Once an appointment has been made, your GP can:

- agree to see your child, with or without you being present
- help encourage your child to acknowledge that there is a problem

- talk about your role in your child's care and treatment

- give you information about NHS treatment options

- talk about treatment options with your child

- provide information about what support is available to you

When this happens you will feel supported, less isolated and more confident about tackling these issues at home. The eating disorder becomes what it is – a serious illness to be treated – not a mysterious secret that no one dares mention.

Some family doctors are more sympathetic and well-informed than others, so be prepared for your first professional encounter to be disappointing. If your child is mature enough for confidentiality to apply, you may never know exactly what transpires during a consultation.

## Useful information and support

Once you and your child seek treatment, beginning with the first appointment, you enter new territory. Prepare for this by making use of any relevant information and support available.

An extremely useful booklet, published by the National Institute for Health and Clinical Excellence (NICE), will give you and your child a good idea of what treatment and care you should expect. It was written chiefly for people with eating disorders. You can obtain a copy from NICE or NHS Direct. This guide summarises and explains the NICE clinical guideline on eating disorders, a substantial work of several hundred pages, produced for NHS healthcare professionals in England and to a limited extent, in Wales. There is also a 'quick reference guide' for professionals in booklet form. EDA also has two leaflets available, one for carers and one for young people, on 'Understanding the NICE Guideline', both of which are free. Do be aware that although clinical guidelines make recommendations to healthcare professionals on the best way of treating conditions, these are not compulsory. It is likely that similar guidelines for Scotland and Northern Ireland will be developed in the future (see the Appendix at the end of the book).

You can call EDA's adult helpline for sources of support for yourself. The Youthline is available for sufferers, friends and siblings who are 18 years old or younger. Contact details can be found at the back of the book.

## The first appointment

If you are making the first appointment, try asking for a double appointment; say what it's about if you can or explain that it's a sensitive issue. You may consider writing to your GP first, to start explaining your concerns. You may feel it is more appropriate for your child to make the appointment and for you to accompany them for support.

If your child is uneasy about talking to a GP, they may feel more comfortable talking to the practice nurse first, but the GP will have to be involved later if a diagnosis is to be made and referrals initiated. Signs of an eating disorder that will be looked for during the first appointment include:

- excessive concern about weight
- with girls, problems with periods
- low weight for their age or recent significant weight loss
- vomiting with no other obvious explanation

Your child may be weighed to find out if they are within a healthy weight range for their age and height and the GP may ask for some blood tests. Conversation might be directed towards identifying signs of depression and low self-esteem.

### HOW CAN YOU HELP?

- Remember that your child's first contact with a professional about the eating disorder will be extremely daunting; your support and encouragement will be vital, whether you are present throughout the consultation, waiting in the car outside, or back at home. A hug or some space might be needed straight afterwards, before there can be any talk. There might be anger, distress, relief or refusal to discuss it at all.

- Talking to the GP or nurse poses a direct threat to the eating disorder and if the *voice* is active your child will be in turmoil, torn between conflicting loyalties. This can make it difficult for a trusting relationship to develop between the health professional and the patient.

- If your child is mature enough to be seen alone and you are not invited to be present, you will feel frustrated that you do not know what is said or how accurately the consultation is reported back. Try not to probe; wait to be told. This will be difficult if the GP either seemed unsympathetic or was so aware of eating disorder issues that your child chose to withhold significant information.

- Although many health professionals are aware of eating disorders, some will be less familiar with them. The GP might not respond immediately to your concerns, perhaps suggesting that this is just 'a phase'; if your child's behaviour is really out of character you should say so. Be clear about your concerns, when the food problems started and what symptoms you have noticed. You may have to become assertive if you feel you are not being listened to.

- If you have written down these details beforehand, you will find it easier to include everything you think relevant during the consultation. Be prepared to be persistent, politely persistent, if you are really worried about your child.

- You may have to make a separate appointment to see the GP on your own. The GP may not be prepared to discuss the consultation with your child, but should be prepared to listen to your concerns and consider them in future consultations with your child.

- If you feel you are not being listened to, it might be worth mentioning your awareness of the NICE guideline. The smaller guide is worth referring to before healthcare appointments: at the back there is a section dedicated to questions you and your child might need to ask.

- Whatever the outcome of the first appointment, remember that for your child this is a momentous event. Make it clear that you realise this. It will also be challenging for you, especially if you were reluctant to talk about the eating disorder to begin with.

● If an appointment is made but your child refuses to attend, either ring to cancel or attend on your own and explain your own concerns and fears. We look at reluctance to accept help later.

## What happens next?

This depends on the severity of the eating disorder: your child may be offered a course of counselling, dietary advice or referral to a specialist for further assessment. Sufferers of bulimia are sometimes offered a self-help programme to follow.

Assessment should be conducted by a professional with specialist experience of treating people with eating disorders. It should include a comprehensive analysis of your child's medical, psychological and social needs, any physical or psychological risks your child may be facing and whether any urgent action is necessary. The specialist may think it appropriate for you to be present throughout the assessment process or believe that this is not in your child's best interest. If your child is seen alone, you may be asked later about your child's condition.

The specialist may ask your child about weight and shape, exercise and food. Information will be needed about your child's personality, social and academic life, any history of dieting or concern about weight, shape or appearance and why you believe your child may have an eating disorder. This background will help to gain an insight into your child's physical and psychological health; it may also reveal factors that might have contributed to the eating disorder. The specialist may also ask for blood and urine tests, check blood pressure and possibly take X-rays or a scan.

If you have had an eating disorder yourself, or you are in recovery, be prepared to find this interview quite distressing. If you do, it is essential that you access support for yourself.

Your GP should still continue to monitor your child's medical and psychological needs, even when other specialists become involved. When more than one healthcare professional is involved in your child's treatment there should be a written agreement or 'care plan' that says who is responsible for checking on the various aspects of your child's health. This agreement should be shared with your child and usually with you, as you are likely to be responsible for getting your child to and from appointments.

Healthcare professionals should also offer information that helps you to care effectively for your child at home: this should cover the nature, course and treatment of the eating disorder as well as general advice on how to support your child, for example what foods they should be eating. You should also be told about any support groups that may be available to you and your family.

What we outline here represents best practice. For some of you and your children the reality may not match this. You might consider keeping dated notes of all appointments and treatment you're involved in.

## Treatment

We consider here the treatment and care that may be offered after assessment, involving healthcare professionals other than your GP. They should discuss any concerns your child or you may have about treatment before it commences.

Your child should expect to be treated as close to where they live as possible, in age-appropriate facilities. However, if there is no specialist service available where you live, treatment may involve some travel. It is usually preferable to receive treatment in a facility where staff are qualified and experienced in treating patients with eating disorders, rather than in general hospitals or general psychiatric clinics. Staff in specialist facilities will be more aware of specific related issues, such as patients' anxiety about mealtimes. This knowledge puts specialist staff in a better position to be able to provide suitable treatment and care. They should also take into account your child's educational and social needs and ensure that these needs are being met while your child receives the best treatment available.

It is important that a supportive and caring relationship is developed between your child and the healthcare professionals who treat them. This should include you and your family if involved in treatment. Mutual respect is the key: the professionals should understand how important a role the family plays in supporting a young person through the treatment process. You should be kept informed about how you and your family can aid the treatment process and provide effective care for your child at home. Ask questions when you do not understand what is said and encourage your child to do the same, so you avoid needless worry and uncertainty at home.

We outline below some forms of treatment that are presently available for people affected by eating disorders. Remember that no two people are the same and what works for one young person may not necessarily work for another. You and the professionals working with your child may need to try several different treatments before you find one that suits the child. The first course of therapy tried is unlikely to ensure complete recovery.

### Anorexia nervosa

Most patients with anorexia will be treated as outpatients or day patients. This means that your child will have appointments at a hospital clinic but will not need to be admitted for overnight care. The professional who sees your child during such appointments should be experienced in delivering this type of treatment. Your child's physical health, including weight, should be monitored during every consultation. A care plan, including dietary advice to follow at home, should be given to your child. You will usually be included in any discussions about meal plans or diet, as this will help you to care more effectively at home. The psychological treatment may last for three to six months initially; however, it is likely to continue for much longer on an outpatient or occasional basis.

If your child is very ill or has a very low weight, it may be necessary for them to be treated in hospital. If they are admitted into hospital, this should be a specialist unit with experience of treating young people of your child's age group who have eating disorders. Ideally this should be within reasonable travelling distance of where you live. This is inpatient treatment. The length of time that your child is in hospital will depend on the severity of their condition.

A central aim of treatment is to help patients reach a safe weight for their height and age by increasing the level of nutrients they are absorbing. Patients treated in hospital or a specialist eating disorders unit will often be set a target weight gain of a half to one kilo a week. Young sufferers of anorexia fear weight gain and it is not uncommon for them to manipulate their weight so that they appear to be meeting the target gain successfully. They can do this by drinking large amounts of water and by hiding heavy objects in their underwear or pockets. Health professionals will usually be aware of this behaviour and know what signs to look for in their young patients when it's time to be weighed. Your child may be given a multivitamin or multimineral supplement.

Psychological therapy should also be an important part of any treatment programme. This should focus on the patients' eating habits, attitudes towards food, weight and shape and the feelings they have in relation to gaining weight. There are many kinds of psychological treatments that have been adapted to treat patients with anorexia, which include:

- Cognitive Analytic Therapy (CAT)
  The therapist works with the young person to help them achieve positive changes in their lives and work towards the future. This therapy helps people to improve the ways in which they cope with their problems.

- Cognitive Behavioural Therapy (CBT)
  The aim is to help young people establish links between their feelings, thoughts or behaviours and their symptoms. Patients may explore different ways of coping with their symptoms and reducing stress. Thoughts, feelings or behaviours connected with the symptoms are often monitored.

- Family Therapy
  This involves the family taking part in sessions with a healthcare professional. This therapy concentrates on the eating disorder, how it affects family relationships and how these relationships may have led to the development of the eating disorder. Sessions may focus on how the family can work together to support each other and work through difficult issues they are facing.

- Focal Psychodynamic Therapy
  The therapist aims to identify and focus on difficulties or conflicts that may have occurred in the early stages of a person's life and which are responsible for their current problems.

- Interpersonal Therapy (IPT)
  This helps patients to identify and address current interpersonal problems, for example low self-esteem.

● Motivational interviewing (MI)

This is a form of cognitive–behavioural technique that aims to help sufferers identify and change behaviours that may be preventing their recovery.

**Other therapies** which may be useful as part of the overall treatment programme include **Art Therapy** and **Drama Therapy** which use art or drama to express emotions that are difficult to talk about. **Reflexology** and **Aromatherapy** help with relaxation and encourage participants to feel good about themselves. However, these therapies will always run alongside the psychological therapies outlined above.

Your child may see a therapist alone, with a group of patients of similar age, or with you and your family. Their treatment may also involve a mixture of the therapeutic approaches we have mentioned.

It is unlikely that your child will be offered any drug therapy for their anorexia. However, if they have associated depression it is possible that if it is very serious, they may receive some medication.

### What if your child refuses to eat?

If a patient's weight is very low and they refuse to eat at all, they may be 'tube fed'. The medical term for this procedure is *enteral tube feeding* or, when the tube is passed through the nose, *naso-gastric feeding*. It involves gently passing a very thin tube up the patient's nose and lowering it into their stomach. The procedure is uncomfortable but not usually painful. Feeds are then passed down the tube. Re-feeding will continue using either a tube feed or with patients feeding themselves; this may be with a liquid feed rather than normal food.

### Anorexia after hospital

Once your child is well enough to leave hospital they should be offered outpatient therapy that continues to focus on their attitudes towards weight and shape, their eating behaviour and social needs. Ideally this therapy should continue until there are no more concerns about their behaviour or health.

Weight gain during treatment should not be confused with a complete recovery. Anorexia can take years to recover from, so professional support should continue after leaving inpatient care. Your child may experience extreme anxiety and stress because of the weight gained in hospital. Maintain the support for them that you have developed at home on a long-term basis. Try to take each day as it comes and avoid unrealistic expectations. It may take several attempts at recovery before your child is successful.

Inpatient treatment may take many weeks, even months. When the therapy team feel your child is ready to leave hospital they should draw up a care plan. Under the terms of the National Service Framework for Mental Health, all carers are entitled to a written care plan when their child leaves hospital. This care plan should offer information on what kind of meals should be eaten, what follow-up support is recommended and what level of exercise is acceptable. If you have any concerns about the care plan, talk to a member of your child's treatment team for advice or more information. The plan must be realistic and reflect your own circumstances. You should be involved in the production of the care plan and you should receive a copy of the plan.

## Bulimia nervosa

Usually young people with bulimia are treated as outpatients. They are rarely admitted into hospital as inpatients, unless they are at risk of suicide, severe self-harm or a medical complication. If your child is vomiting frequently or using excessive amounts of laxatives, your GP or healthcare professional may want them to have a blood test. This is necessary as some people with bulimia can suffer from dehydration and chemical imbalances that can be detected in the blood. If left untreated, such conditions can result in heart disease and other physical problems.

If the patient is female, an examination of the ovaries might be carried out, as bulimia can cause the development of polycystic ovarian syndrome (POS). This is a condition that can affect a woman's menstrual cycle, fertility, insulin production, hormones, heart, blood vessels and appearance. Women with POS usually develop the following characteristics:

- an irregular or no menstrual cycle

- high levels of male hormones, usually referred to as androgens, which may lead to development of male pattern hair growth

- small cysts, which are fluid-filled sacs, on their ovaries

In serious cases your child may be prescribed a form of antidepressant medication. This may be a 'Selective Serotonin Reuptake Inhibitor' (SSRI). One of the most commonly used antidepressants used to treat bulimia is Fluoxetine (Prozac). This and other antidepressants work by correcting abnormalities in the neurotransmitters in the brain cells. Neurotransmitters are the chemical messengers in the brain. This treatment can help to reduce the urge to binge eat. Antidepressants should not replace psychiatric treatment and are used very much less than they used to be because of serious concerns about their effect on children (see the NICE guidelines on the treatment of depression in children and young adults).

Your child should be offered several months of psychological treatment during outpatient care. Young people with bulimia may be offered a course of cognitive behavioural therapy especially adapted for bulimia nervosa (CBT-BN). This course of treatment usually involves a number of one-to-one and group sessions. The treatment will focus on helping the patient to recognise what triggers the compulsion to binge eat and purge. The therapist will work with the patient to develop strategies to overcome these trigger factors. Patients will be shown ways of re-evaluating their perceptions of themselves by challenging the negative thoughts they have in relation to their body and self-esteem. This form of treatment may include you and your family if thought appropriate. Other possible treatment options are mentioned in the section on treatment for anorexia.

## Binge eating disorder (BED)

Young sufferers who have binge eating disorder are usually treated as outpatients. However, they may be asked to attend specialist day units where they will be advised about planning and eating healthy meals. Antidepressants may be prescribed; as with bulimia, this medication can reduce the urge to binge eat, but antidepressants are much less commonly used in young patients because of concerns about serious side effects.

Outpatients may be offered a course of psychological treatment that lasts for several months. Therapies used in the treatment of BED include:

- Cognitive behaviour therapy especially adapted for binge eating disorder

- Interpersonal psychotherapy

Healthcare professionals should ensure that any psychological treatment offered is appropriate to the individual needs and age of your child. As with anorexia, art and drama therapy or reflexology and aromatherapy may be offered alongside psychological treatment.

### Atypical eating disorder or 'eating disorder not otherwise specified' (EDNOS)

Either term may be used if your child has an eating disorder that does not meet the precise criteria of anorexia, bulimia or binge eating disorder. In such cases healthcare professionals will normally follow the guidance available for the eating disorder that is most similar to the one from which your child is suffering. Your child's individual needs, circumstances and age should all be considered when healthcare professionals are deciding on what treatment would be most appropriate. Atypical eating disorders or EDNOS are the most common form of disorders; nevertheless this term does not mean that this type of eating disorder is less serious.

## Fear of help

When treatment and care are offered you will feel some relief but potential hazards lie ahead. Real fear of help may be projected as sullen compliance or fierce resistance. If this chapter is relevant to you now, remind yourself and your child that you have already made significant progress since you first wondered if something was wrong.

You might like to refer back to Chapter One at some point and remind yourself about the powerful *voice* that is the jealous enemy of recovery. We also described the stages of change experienced as your child recovers from an eating disorder; the stage your child has reached will affect reactions to any form of treatment or care. Even the stage of determination and action can falter when the reality of treatment is felt. Fear of help is really fear of change, change that will result in loss of the eating disorder – an alarming prospect.

## HOW CAN YOU HELP?

- Teach your child to recognise and challenge the *voice*. Fighting the *voice* will be hard work for you: maintain your own preferred support systems, but be open to fresh approaches such as attending a self-help group for carers or reading books with recovery as the main theme. Look again at the booklist on the EDA website or visit your local bookshops or library.

- If your child is fearful about treatment, especially when weight gain is involved, suggest they call the EDA Youthline. You might find the message board useful for an insight into the fear that makes eating disorders so difficult to treat.

- Give praise for courage shown in accepting and persisting with treatment. Ask your child to tell you when they feel pleased with small but significant achievements.

- Encourage your child to give healthcare professionals and treatment a decent chance and ask that advice is not dismissed automatically; your example will be important. There will be attempts to wear you down with arguments for stopping treatment and angry tirades about how pointless and stupid it is. Remain patient and explore positive reasons for continuing. Don't be afraid to reaffirm your belief that treatment is necessary.

- Try not to jump to any conclusions about the treatment and care your child is receiving. It is important not to dismiss complaints but be aware that accounts may be embellished in the hope that further treatment can be avoided. Ask what is so upsetting and explore these issues together. You might offer to talk to healthcare professionals with your child but remember that many therapists will prefer to talk to the child alone. If the concerns are not valid, your child is unlikely to push the issue any further. Remember that lying and emotional blackmail are symptoms of the illness so try not to take this personally: it's part of the sufferer's drive to maintain the eating disorder.

## What if your child refuses treatment?

If your child is dangerously ill but refuses treatment, action can be taken to ensure that treatment is given and the patient detained in hospital if necessary. Young people can be 'sectioned' under the Mental Health Act (1985) or, if under the age of 18, the Children Act (1989) or Children (Scotland) Act (1995). The term 'sectioned' refers to treatment given as specified by a particular section of the relevant act. This means that at least two healthcare professionals have decided that treatment is in the best interests of the person concerned. Sectioning is rare and should only be used as a last resort when the person is far too ill to make rational decisions about their own treatment. It is a difficult and stressful process for everyone involved, but it can also be a huge relief.

## Confidentiality and family involvement

If your child is under 16 years of age, many healthcare professionals will be prepared to see you with them during some consultations. There are circumstances when a healthcare professional will consult with a young person under 16 without their parents' knowledge, but this happens only if the young person is considered to be mature enough and well enough to understand and agree to treatment on their own. Most healthcare professionals will want to work with the patient's family and encourage their involvement in treatment. Nevertheless, it is quite common for specialists to insist that the first few sessions are with the patient alone. Occasionally the professional may consider family involvement inappropriate if it could put the patient at greater risk, or perhaps where abuse of some kind is suspected.

If your child is 16 years of age or older they are usually responsible for making their own decisions about treatment in the NHS. However, if healthcare professionals feel that a patient's health is deteriorating rapidly they may decide to inform family members of the situation, regardless of the patient's age. Even if you do not have an active role in your child's treatment programme, you should be offered enough information to help you provide adequate care for your child at home. This means that you should be told about your child's progress in treatment and expect to be included in discussions about the care plan and other issues such as meal plans.

Family involvement in treatment is often extremely positive for the young person. Consistent love and support can really boost and maintain morale. Some healthcare professionals will offer therapy that involves the whole family, while others may want your child to be seen alone, which can make you feel shut out. If they do want to see your child alone, try not to take offence at this. It might just be what your child needs at this particular time. Put your energies into supporting them at home or into your role as visitor when inpatient treatment is necessary.

## Going into hospital.

Going into hospital for the first time can be very traumatic for anyone, but especially for a young person leaving behind the comfort and familiarity of home. Because of this and their reluctance to shed their disorder, at this stage it is normal for staff to ask parents not to make contact for the first few days as the patient will use every excuse to avoid treatment in much the same way as they would to avoid eating. For the same reason they may ban mobile phones; if this is the case do make sure your child complies with this request.

It is possible that your child may nevertheless telephone you to tell you how badly they are being treated and how important it is that you collect them as soon as possible. The call may be accompanied by many tears and a lot of emotional blackmail. This distressing call is quite a common occurrence and should be firmly ignored. Because it may be very upsetting you might wish to call the unit and discuss it with the professionals. They are likely to confirm that this is a normal response to beginning treatment and should be ignored, or they may suggest a response you should use in any future calls.

## What if you are not happy with the treatment?

If you are not happy with the treatment that your child is receiving, you should always try to address the problem with the relevant healthcare professionals first. They may be extremely helpful and responsive. If not, you could consider asking your GP for help.

Alternatively, you can contact the Patient Advice and Liaison Service (PALS). This service is available in all NHS trusts. Information about how to contact PALS is at the back of the book. This service offers:

● information on the NHS and health issues

● confidential advice and support to patients, families and carers

● confidential assistance in resolving concerns and problems quickly

● information on NHS complaints procedures and who can help

● information on how young people can become more involved in their own healthcare

If these approaches are unsuccessful, you can write to the Chief Executive of the Mental Health Trust and to your MP, who will respond to your complaint. If you feel the situation has still not been resolved, then you could ask for outside help. A specialist mental health social worker can challenge a decision about treatment with the Department of Health. You can find out more about this from your local Social Security office.

Be very wary of allowing your child to know about your concerns. If you devalue their treatment or constantly question it, this may be used as an excuse for refusing or discontinuing treatment. There is no magic wand that a specialist team can wave to cure your child. Finding the most appropriate treatment may take time and patience. Even during professional treatment your child's progress may slow down, and of course occasionally speed up. However, if you are concerned about continuing deterioration you should talk to a member of the treatment team.

## After treatment

Even after your child has regained their physical health, your continued support at home will be needed. This includes encouragement to continue with any professional support that has been offered, which can be outpatient care, counselling or attendance at a support group. This stage of an eating disorder is 'maintenance', which can be extremely difficult and frustrating for your child and for the family, which is why follow-up support is so important.

Recovery is a long, slow process, which can easily be threatened. Your child's emotional health is just as important as their physical health: it takes time to help your child to develop positive ways of coping with the difficult emotions that the eating disorder helped them to control. Be patient and praise every positive step along the way, however small; prepare yourself for setbacks. At times when your child is feeling low, the *voice* may return and be difficult to resist. You should accept all the support you are offered in the fight for recovery.

## Recent developments

The development of treatment for eating disorders is a slow process. Research into these complex disorders tends to reveal ways in which small advances can be made rather than revealing giant leaps forward. Nevertheless, there are many dedicated people constantly assessing new ways to help people with eating disorders and reassessing existing therapies. One form of treatment that is currently being assessed is computer-based CD ROM and internet based therapy. This type of therapy only appeals to, and works for, some people but it does allow them to work on their own and at their own pace. If they are motivated to follow the course to its conclusion, the outcomes seem to be positive.

## CHAPTER SEVEN

# Recovery

You will be delighted to see your child beginning to recover, but recovery is a complex process; pace yourself and muster all the support available for you, your child and your family. You have endured more than you ever thought possible; you have become much stronger emotionally. We hope you understand now why addressing your own needs is an important responsibility.

## Recovering slowly

For recovery to be possible the sufferer must accept that there is a problem and want change. Coming out of denial is difficult enough: in some cases it doesn't happen. A real desire for change, the conviction that life could be better without the eating disorder, is even harder to acquire; much time can pass before the stage of 'determination and action' is reached. However loving, understanding and patient you are, this is where your parental influence stops; your child must reach this stage by themselves if recovery is to be a realistic ambition. Even after inpatient treatment, recovery can be extremely fragile as the return home can soon reveal.

> *I think my daughter found things really hard after hospital. She hated the fact that she had gained weight and didn't know how she would feel once she was home again. She wanted to exercise straight away and her food problems were a long way off being over. She was confused and stuck somewhere between wanting to get well and hanging on to her eating disorder as it was what she knew best.* DENISE

*I want to get well, but I don't want to eat 'normally' either…If I push myself a little more each day, I hope that eventually I will be strong enough to fight my eating disorder. I will also have my family to help me. They may never completely understand, but they love me.* SHANNON

Denise's daughter and Shannon share the conflict common to sufferers once their eating disorder problems have been admitted: they fear change in their eating habits and they dread the inevitable weight gain. Denise must have been so pleased when her daughter finally received treatment but the return home was confusing and difficult for them both. Shannon knows he is not yet ready to take action on recovery, but his determination is growing. Denise is obviously a supportive parent and Shannon knows that when he is strong enough to embark on recovery he will be supported by his parents.

## HOW CAN YOU HELP?

- Accept that recovery is as complex as the eating disorder and that disillusionment with the illness does not necessarily mean that your child is ready to fight it.

- Understand that weight gain will distress your child however keen the desire for change. Weight gain in itself simply means that your child is eating more, but it does not indicate real recovery unless there is psychological change too, which will be evident when food becomes less of an issue and when weight gain is accepted as an essential part of the recovery process.

- Young people recovering from binge eating disorder, compulsive eating and some cases of bulimia will also have difficulties as they try to treat food in a normal way.

- You may need to prepare relatives and close friends for the uncertainties of recovery. Untold damage can be done with comments on the lines of 'You look much better now you've filled out a bit!' or 'Well, lose another two stone and you'll look as good as your sister!' or 'Here's a box of chocolates – you deserve it for doing so well!'

- Sometimes even praising a small change can present difficulties for the sufferer as they may feel they have failed their eating disorder and react in unexpected ways.

● Recognise the truth of Shannon's comments that parental love and support is really appreciated and will be needed when the will for change is found.

## Two steps forward, one step back

Try not to be disappointed if your child appears to be recovering well from their eating disorder and then either reverts to old behaviours or just seems to come to a standstill.

It can take years to recover from an eating disorder and sometimes many attempts at recovery may be needed. Try to see even the wish for change as a positive step and regard any real change as a major achievement, even if short-lived. If you and your child can think of 'two steps forward, one step back' as good recovery, perhaps you can accept more disappointing variations as normal for recovery from eating disorders.

> *My daughter was back and forth to appointments for her bulimia all of the time. Her disorder was very extreme so we were constantly hoping for signs of improvement in her condition to ease our concern. When she made any improvement we thought we had got what we were hoping for and were so overwhelmingly happy. However, sometimes this improvement was short lived and then we would have to face disappointment. I think sometimes it can be best not to set your hopes too high and just live day to day. Stay positive and never give up hope, but don't expect miracle solutions!* SHARON

Sharon was desperate for signs of recovery but made the understandable mistake of believing that any improvement in her daughter's condition would be permanent. This caused disappointment when the bulimia took over yet again. Her daughter will have felt terrible, on her own account and on behalf of her family. Gradually this family learned that recovery comes in fits and starts. Constant steady progress is unlikely.

Some aspects of recovery from anorexia are alarming but normal. Hair loss, for example, is common, but as patients recover their hair will grow properly again.

Many sufferers will lose friends, sometimes even close friends, who can't cope with the changes brought on by the disorder. Your child will need additional support if they have no circle of friends to turn to. Although it may not be easy, they should be encouraged to make contact with old friends, many of whom will be pleased to renew an old friendship.

Occasionally sufferers may come across 'Pro-anorexia' or 'Pro-bulimia' websites that are run by sufferers still deeply entrenched in an eating disorder. These sites encourage the view that an eating disorder is a *lifestyle choice* and actively discourage recovery. If you think your child is being influenced by these sites be prepared to challenge their negative viewpoint. It is probably unhelpful to try banning them from visiting the sites as this will only lead to secrecy and deceit as they seek other ways to access the sites away from home.

## HOW CAN YOU HELP?

- If you are realistic, without being a killjoy, it will be easier for your child to cope with setbacks. Use terms like 'setback' or 'one step back' rather than allowing talk of 'failure', which will lower everyone's morale. Remember we all learn from our mistakes and a setback may be an opportunity to try something else.

- Make it easy for your child to talk about the negative aspects of recovery; such conversations are in themselves a blow against the *voice*, which will be heard loud and clear whenever there's a step or two backwards. However, also remember to make space for conversations about recovery when things are going well. You don't want to give the impression that once your child seems to have recovered you will lose interest.

- Ask how you can help when recovery is difficult, when the urge to binge, to purge, to exercise obsessively or to limit calorie intake is strong.

- Prepare friends and relatives for the problems with recovery. Talk of 'recovering' or being 'in recovery' but avoid the word 'recovered'.

- Bear in mind that a new self-help book or different form of therapy may suggest a new or different approach, but don't rush such changes in case the real problem is simply fear of recovery and its implications.

## Living without the eating disorder

When someone has been dependent on an eating disorder for a long time, the prospect of living without it can be frightening. After all, this has been their coping strategy of choice whenever life has been too painful to bear.

*Things will be different though, as I won't have my bulimia to fall back on when things get tough.* LAURA

Here Laura, whose thoughts are included at the end of Chapter One, is contemplating her return to school but reveals some anxiety; she knows that she will experience normal frustrations and disappointments head on so new coping strategies will be needed. Many emotions will be strongly felt by Laura without the distractions of her old bulimic behaviours deadening their impact.

When your child seems well enough to return to education or work, you may wish to spend some time exploring what is available in the way of support for them. Although your child may be keen to return, their enthusiasm may be greater than their capacity to cope with the reality of catching up with missed work. They may also find that mealtimes are fraught with difficulties, especially if they still rely heavily on set routines and habits.

Another problem for young people in recovery is loss of identity. They have been defined by the eating disorder for so long that they may no longer be quite sure who they are, what they want from this new life or how to relate to others. Parents can lose their way, too, and may have their own identity crisis; as their child recovers and perhaps becomes more assertive and independent, parents can feel lost, almost rejected, because they have been so used to their role as carers.

## HOW CAN YOU HELP?

● Recovery can bring to the surface difficult feelings, which the eating disorder has blocked for so long. Be prepared for your child to go through a whole range of different emotions; explain that these emotions are natural and normal, although uncomfortable.

● Encourage openness about what is provoking the anger, jealousy or anxiety. You may have to work with your child to recognise and identify different emotions and sensations. Be prepared to talk about your own feelings and how you cope with them.

● Be prepared for obvious stressful flashpoints such as making choices about GCSE or A-level examination subjects, waiting for results or applying for a place at university. On a more personal level, relationship upsets will be a real test of recovery. There will also be the daily challenges that involve food and the casual conversations about appearance and weight that crop up so often at school, in the media and elsewhere.

- Keep a balance in conversation topics at home. Introduce matters of interest to you and your partner, siblings and the family as a whole, as well as giving your child freedom to talk about recovery problems.

- This is asking a lot, but try to regain your sense of humour and help your child, gently, to rediscover the sense of fun they had before they became so ill. When you've managed this, perhaps you can even begin to laugh at the *voice*. This will help your child feel more in control.

- Encourage your child to keep a note somewhere of tiny achievements and make this a topic of conversation regularly. If you've been keeping a diary, continue with it.

## What if your child doesn't recover?

With the right help and support, most young people will recover from their eating disorder and go on to live healthy, fulfilling lives. Some will struggle with their eating disorder off and on throughout their lives, but will overcome the most dangerous difficulties with food by relying on coping strategies learned during treatment. Of course if the eating disorder is not recognised, acknowledged or treated it can have fatal consequences. Remember that early intervention with young people makes recovery much more likely.

*My daughter has struggled with her anorexia for many years now. At the moment she seems to be doing OK, but I know there is always a chance that she will slip back into it again. I also know in the back of my mind that if she did and things got really bad, there is a small chance that she could die as a result of it. As a parent, I think that it is really important to accept the fact that you cannot control your child's eating disorder or their recovery. You can support them as much as possible, but you cannot do it for them. I think you need to adopt a positive but realistic way of thinking when it comes to your child's illness. Harness your energy into loving them as much as you can, and remember that you cannot save them, you can only support them.* MICHAEL

Michael has had to accept a harsh truth: he is unable to ensure his daughter's survival. This is true in a sense for all parents. However healthy and happy our children are, none of us has the power to protect them from all harm. Some readers will have children who have incurable conditions; they have had to find a way to live with this.

## HOW CAN YOU HELP?

- It is important to accept that you are not in control of your child's eating disorder and therefore you cannot ensure recovery because only your child can find the will to change. What you can do is put your energies into supporting them at home with encouragement, common sense, a few boundaries and much unconditional love. As long as you do this, you are meeting your responsibilities as a parent and doing all that you can for them.

- Refer back to earlier chapters if you need some guidance on how you might best support your child and yourself.

- Try to keep a positive attitude for the child who is ill and for the rest of your family. This is not an easy task, but you will increase the chances of your child developing a healthy outlook if you set a good example and have one yourself. This does not mean that you have to hide any negative feelings you may have; try to have several outlets for these feelings so they are released regularly and safely.

- There are books written specifically about recovery and its attendant problems, including the possibility that some sufferers may not recover in the sense of returning to a full and healthy life. You might find these of help if you are feeling despondent. Look through the sources of support listed at the end of this chapter. There is a useful booklist on the EDA website.

- However bleak the outlook seems to you at times, you must not give up hope, not if you want your child to find the will to stay alive and fight the illness. Try to maintain that sense of normality, however elusive it seems. Keep your child in touch with the real world in any way possible, even though the private world of the eating disorder is so powerful. You may need counselling to help you deal with this situation.

## Long-term support

Maintaining long-term support is vital for anyone who has recovered from an eating disorder. Even several years after recovery it can be easy, without support, to slip back into the comfort of the eating disorder.

*Our son still needs encouragement when it comes to battling his eating disorder. He has been recovered for years, but still has his good days and bad days. We try to keep a positive attitude when he has a bad day, as we want him to know that it is OK to admit to feeling unable to cope. I am just glad that he feels he can talk to us about things.* CHARLIE

Charlie accepts the inevitability of 'good days and bad days' and, most importantly, his son knows he doesn't have to pretend that all is well when it isn't.

### HOW CAN YOU HELP?

- Keep the lines of communication open, whether your child is living with you at home or away. The simple question 'How are you?' can be asked in such a way that your child knows you are really interested. Let it be an open question; don't immediately follow it with questions about meals, weight and exercise! Listen to the reply and pursue the concerns that are expressed.

- If you have fears that recovery is faltering, mention this calmly; suggest a call or text to the EDA Youthline if your concerns seem to be shared.

- Remember to tell your child that you love them and let them know that you admire their hard work towards recovery. Encouragement and positive reinforcement are often overlooked when a person regains their health.

- Is there counselling or a support group that might help with maintaining recovery? (Very few self-help groups accept young people under 18.) Perhaps there are books that might be helpful with this stage; encourage your child to look for the booklist on the EDA website.

Recovery can be a very stressful experience for the young sufferer but it can also be a very stressful experience for the rest of the family. Your child will experience a bewildering range of emotions as they slowly learn to cope without the eating disorder. This will inevitably stir up emotions in other members of the family, especially if resentments have simmered beneath the surface for some time.

Sometimes parents believe that they are not entitled to support any longer because the young person is recovering and has regained physical health. However, they are likely to be working towards emotional recovery for some time. This means that they will still require support and so will their family.

> *When my child had regained her physical health, I thought our problems were over and stopped the support I had in place for myself. I was wrong to rush into this though because I learnt very quickly that my daughter's food problems were not over. She needed as much support as she always did which meant that I needed some outside help as well.* SUZANNE

## HOW CAN YOU HELP?

- Don't rush to change the routines and activities that you put in place when your child was physically ill. These will provide a sense of stability for you and your family and will help all of you to cope more effectively with the emotional challenges you may yet have to face. Refer back to earlier chapters and to other self-help books for more ideas.

- Remember that it is not just your child who needs outside support – you all do. Support can be personal, within the immediate family unit or from friends and relatives. It can also be professional: we have suggested many forms of support throughout the book. You will find contact details and other possibilities in the last few pages. Do make use of them.

## A learning experience

Coping with your child's eating disorder has probably been bewildering, frightening, frustrating and exhausting. You will have other words to add to that list and most of them may seem negative, especially if you are reading this on a bad day.

We tend to assume that we learn from experience automatically, but perhaps we have to make a conscious effort to do so. Remember that you and your family have probably learnt much of lasting value about yourselves as individuals, about each other and about the way you all cope under difficult circumstances. Try not to disregard this information once you feel your child has recovered. Keep supporting each other and keep talking. Try to draw out the positive things that you and your family have learned from this experience and use them in your everyday lives to help each other.

We conclude with the words of the young people we featured earlier:

*Recovery taught me so much about myself. I learned about the people I love, the person I am and how much I want to live and be happy. These are the things I am going to hang on to.* PAUL

*I hope that one day I will be happy with myself and enjoy eating, rather than dreading it.* REBECCA

*I will also have my family to help me. They may never completely understand, but they love me.* SHANNON

*I am determined to get control of my life, I don't want the eating disorder to win and that is what keeps me positive.* SIMONE

*My parents helped me get through my bulimia. They loved and supported me during some difficult times. There were many times when I threw their love and support right back in their faces…Somewhere along the way I became friends with them again and saw that they were trying to look out for me…I need to cope on my own in better ways, but luckily my parents will be there to encourage and support me when I need them.* LAURA

# Useful contacts

## Eating Disorders Association (EDA)

Please note, EDA may be changing its name during 2006. However, all the website and telephone contacts below will continue to work.

EDA is a national charity that offers information, support and understanding about eating disorders and surrounding issues for sufferers, carers and professionals. EDA supports a UK-wide network of self-help groups and offers a wide range of other services including many booklets and leaflets on different aspects of eating disorders.

- **Telephone helpline (adults): 0845 634 1414**
  e-mail: helpmail@edauk.com

- **Youthline (up to 18 years of age): 0845 634 7650**
  e-mail: talkback@edauk.com or text the youth team on 07 977 493 345

- **Minicom service: 01603 753322**
  Open in office hours

- **Website: www.edauk.com**

- **Self-help network.** For further information visit the EDA website or if you don't have access to the internet, please call the Helplines.

You can write to EDA at this address:

Eating Disorders Association
Wensum House
103 Prince of Wales Road
Norwich NR1 1DW

e-mail: info@edauk.com
Admin office: 0870 770 3256
Fax: 01603 664915

## Other organisations

Some of the organisations below only have information available on their website. If you don't have access to the internet yourself, you can use the internet facilities at your local library or perhaps visit an internet cafe. Don't be embarrassed about asking for help.

### Support for carers and parents

### Carers Information

This is a source of information and resources about issues relevant to carers and those professionals who assist them in their role.
website: www.carersinformation.org.uk

### Carers UK

Carers UK is an information and campaigning organisation for carers
Carers UK, 20–25 Glasshouse Yard, London EC1A 4JT
CarersLine: Tel 0808 808 7777
website: www.carersuk.org

### Caring about Carers

Government information for carers in the UK
website: www.carers.gov.uk

## Contact a Family

Contact a Family is a UK-wide charity providing advice, information and support to the parents of all disabled children, no matter what their health condition.
Contact a Family, 209-211 City Road, London EC1V 1JN
Helpline: 0808 808 3555
website: www.cafamily.org.uk

## Crossroads

Crossroads-Caring for Carers, is the leading provider of practical support for Carers in England and Wales. The objective of Crossroads is to give carers time to be themselves, by enabling them to take a much needed short break from their caring responsibilities.
Crossroads Association 10 Regent Place, Rugby Warwickshire CV21 2PN
Helpdesk: 0845 4500350
Website: www.crossroads.org.uk

## Institute of Psychiatry (IoP)

The IoP Eating Disorders Unit website includes information for carers and opportunities to take part in research.
website:
www.iop.kcl.ac.uk/IoP/Departments/PsychMed/EDU/index.shtml

## Parentline Plus

Parentline Plus is a national charity that works for, and with, parents especially when family life becomes challenging and difficult.
Parentline Plus: 0808 800 2222
website: www.parentlineplus.org.uk

## Princess Royal Trust for Carers

Princess Royal Trust for Carers is the largest provider of comprehensive carers' support services in the UK through its unique network of 122 independently managed Carers' Centres and interactive websites.
London Office,142 Minories, London EC3N 1LB
Tel: 020 7480 7788
website: www.carers.org

## *Work-related, grants and general support*

### Citizens Advice Bureau (CAB)

CAB provides free information and independent advice on your rights on a wide range of issues including benefits, housing, employment, debt, consumer and legal matters from nearly 3,400 locations around the UK.
website: www.citizensadvice.org.uk

### Advisory Consultation and Arbitration Service (ACAS)

ACAS provides independent information and advice about employment issues.
website: www.acas.org.uk
Tel: 08457 47 47 47

### Department of Trade and Industry (DTI)

The DTI provide useful information about employment issues and resolving employment problems.
Department of Trade and Industry, Response Centre, 1 Victoria Street, London SW1H 0ET
website: www.dti.gov.uk/er/index.htm

### Department for Work and Pensions

Information about the Carer's Allowance (CA) that is administered by the Carer's Allowance Unit.
CA Unit, Palatine House, Lancaster Road, Preston, Lancashire PR1 1NS
Tel: 01253 856 123
website: www.dwp.gov.uk/lifeevent/benefits/carers_allowance.asp

## *Health – or treatment-related support*

### NHS Direct

Information and advice about any aspect of health or the NHS.
Tel: 0845 4647
website: www.nhsdirect.nhs.uk

### National Institute for Health and Clinical Excellence (NICE)

NICE is responsible for drawing up and publishing the treatment guidelines for a number of disorders and illnesses including eating disorders, self-harm, depression and obsessive-compulsive disorder.

website: www.nice.org.uk and click on the 'Our Guidance' button for the full list of guidelines.

Many guidelines including the eating disorders guideline include a 'quick reference guide' for healthcare professionals and versions for patients or carers.

Copies of guideline booklets can be ordered free by phone from 0870 1555 455.

(Note that NICE guidelines apply to England only. The Scottish Intercollegiate Guidelines Network (SIGN) www.show.scot.nhs.uk/sign/ produces the equivalent Scottish guidelines. At the time of going to press there were no guidelines, or plans for guidelines, on eating disorders or any related topics. There are currently no equivalent organisations for Wales or Northern Ireland although the Welsh health authorities have adopted the 2004 eating disorder guideline.)

### Patient Advisory Liaison Service (PALS)

The Patient Advice and Liaison Service is part of the government's commitment to ensuring that the NHS listens to patients, resolves their immediate concerns and then uses these views to develop services. Call your local hospital, clinic, GP surgery or health centre to ask for details of PALS or call: NHS Direct on 0845 4647.

### *Related disorders*

### National Self-Harm Network (NSHN)

Information and support for people affected by self-harming
PO Box 16190, London NW1 3WW
website: www.nshn.co.uk
NICE (see above) have also published treatment guidelines for self-harm.

## OCD Action

OCD Action is the leading national charity for people with obsessive compulsive disorders and the related disorders of body dysmorphic disorder (BDD).
22/24 Highbury Grove, Suite 107, London N5 2EA
Helpline: 0845 390 6232
website: www.ocdaction.org.uk

### *Information and support for children and young people*

## Childline

Childline is the free helpline for children and young people in the UK. Children and young people can call to talk about any problem.
Childline, FREEPOST 1111, London N1 0BR
Childine: 0800 1111 (24 hours, 7 days a week)
website: www.childline.org.uk

## National Society for the Prevention of Cruelty to Children (NSPCC)

NSPCC is the UK's leading charity specialising in child protection and the prevention of cruelty to children.
Helpline: 0808 800 5000
website: www.nspcc.org.uk

## The Young Carers Initiative

The Young Carers Initiative is part of The Children's Society. They offer information and training to young carers and anyone who works with young carers and their families across England and the UK.
website: www.youngcarer.com